"Derrik does a maste
having faith and *acting on* faith. 'Faith is not a noun, Faith is a verb.' For many people, faith is akin to hoping that everything will work out. Derrik's story embodies that only through our *actions* to give up control and step into God's will are truly free to live."

—Scott T. Rupp, Former Missouri State Senator

"My involvement with the Kassebaum family since 1980 has allowed me to observe the amazing favor of God that still blesses their lives. Derrik's heart for God is influencing so many for the Kingdom of God—many more than he probably realizes. Now his simple story of 'letting go' shows us the wisdom of his faith and the rewards of his obedience.

This book will challenge you, as it has done me, to trust God with the principle that dying to self guarantees a resurrection to new and untold adventures to those who do so. May you be stirred, encouraged, and dared in your faith to 'Live and Let Go' as you read Derrik's honest and humble story."

—Mike Stevens, International Speaker and
Life Development Coach
Mikestevens.world

"One of my favorite passages in the Bible is found in Isaiah 43:18-19: 'Forget the former things; do not dwell on the past. See, I am doing a new thing, now it springs up; do you not perceive it?' For God to do something new in our life, we need to let go of where we are. This is not always easy. In his new book, *Live and Let Go*, Derrik walks us through how God has used his experiences of letting go to grow his faith, increase his trust, and deepen his walk. Derrik's heart for Christ shines through in his writing as he shares personal, authentic stories that teach us the life-changing benefits of letting go and surrendering to God's will."

—Lisa Nichols, CEO and Co-founder Technology Partners

"The principles and lessons Derrik outlines in *Live and Let Go* are ones that can benefit everyone whether it be in business, relationships, or life! I found myself constantly relating to the chapters and stories that were so similar to my life. As a professional baseball player and retiring at twenty-eight years old, I naturally thought, 'OK what's next?' I related to many of the steps and following the doors that continued to open, just like the ones written in this book. Thank you, Derrik, for sharing your journey with us and offering so many learning lessons along the way. I respect you and your family for your obedience and following your calling to make sure you are doing what you've been called to do to the max!"

—Kyle McClellan, Former MLB Cardinals Pitcher
and World Series Champion
Founder and President of Brace for Impact 46

"I have two daughters, ages thirteen and ten, and conversations about boys have already taken place at the dinner table. The scars of the author's great stories are lessons that have empowered me to better accompany my daughters and the hundreds of young people and adults whom I have the privilege of influencing each year as a leader in Guatemala. From the adventure of building a tree house to building a large successful corporation, from the emotions of losing a loved one to seeing your children make transcendent decisions, from imagining an apple speaking to a branch to the God of the universe whispering in you ear—from beginning to end this book will enrich the process of living fully."

—Jose Carrera, Director of Centro De Crecimiento Integral
Pastor and Author of *Starting Point*

LIVE
—AND—
LET GO

LIVE
—AND—
LET GO

Releasing Your Hold to Pursue God's Purpose

Derrik Kassebaum

Stonebrook Publishing
Saint Louis, Missouri

A STONEBROOK PUBLISHING BOOK

©2022 Derrik Kassebaum

This book was guided in development and
edited by Nancy L. Erickson, The Book Professor®
TheBookProfessor.com

All Scripture quotations, unless otherwise indicated, are taken from the Holy Bible, New International Version®, NIV®. Copyright ©1973, 1978, 1984, 2011 by Biblica, Inc.™ Used by permission of Zondervan. All rights reserved worldwide. www.zondervan.comThe "NIV" and "New International Version" are trademarks registered in the United States Patent and Trademark Office by Biblica, Inc.™

Scripture taken from the New King James Version®. Copyright © 1982 by Thomas Nelson. Used by permission. All rights reserved.

Library of Congress Control Number: 2022905575

Paperback ISBN: 978-1-955711-14-2

www.stonebrookpublishing.net

PRINTED IN THE UNITED STATES OF AMERICA

DEDICATION

To my wife Laura, you are truly my best friend, my confidante, and the one who has stood by my side even when it was not deserved. Thank you for being my wife and the love of my life, and the person who shows me Jesus through your actions again and again. I'm so excited to see what God does through us in these next years of our life.

To my daughter, Elise, for making me a father. You're such a strong, amazing woman, and I love that you desire to be all that God has for you. Thank you for continuing to love me and desiring to build a strong relationship with me. I am so, so proud of you and your desire to see all that is beautiful in the world.

To my daughter, Raquel. I love to see the woman you've become and your heart to run after God. I love your adventure of trying so many things in life and going for all that God has for you. I couldn't be prouder of the woman you've become. You absolutely amaze me in all you do.

Thanks to all three of you for putting up with my oddities, my stupid dad jokes, and the growth that each of you have walked through with me. I love you all so much!

CONTENTS

PREFACE

When I was a young boy, we lived out in the country on a gravel road. Our home was surrounded by both a thick wooded area and pastureland for farmers to raise livestock and grow crops. My five siblings and I had plenty of room to explore and live a free, wandering childhood. We also had plenty of opportunity to get ourselves in trouble for doing things we weren't supposed to do, or worse, to physically injure ourselves.

Growing up in the outdoors taught me many things that I carried with me later in life. One life lesson I learned was that life was really about *letting go*. Sometimes letting go was painful and hard and came with a lesson about how to do it better next time. Other times, letting go was a painful but necessary part of life that I had to experience in order to live the life I wanted to live. As a young boy, I learned many sides of this letting go process.

I was an extremely adventurous young boy with a very creative mind. I hated school but loved the outdoors and all the outdoors allowed me to do. I had a hard time following rules because that put restraints on my creativity and the things I wanted to push myself to do. Having older siblings who were similar in this adventurous mindset didn't help me stick to the rules either.

One life lesson I learned was that life was really about letting go.

Being surrounded by woods and farmland gave us great opportunities to explore, hunt, fish, and build treehouses and forts. Years earlier, before I was old enough to enjoy it, my older siblings and my dad had built a two-story treehouse that overlooked a small pond we had for fishing. I was never allowed to go up in it because I was too young. By the time I was old enough to climb in, it was unstable and off-limits.

However, I was determined to build another one with my younger brother so that we, too, could have the adventures that our older siblings had enjoyed. But first, I had to come up with the materials and a place to build it. The place I chose was right outside a wooden fence that surrounded our yard. Because I was only seven years old, I wasn't allowed outside that fence when my parents weren't home.

My parents were very busy, not only with work but also with rehabbing a duplex that they rented out. The only time they had to do the renovation work was on the weekends and during the evenings after Dad got off work—the very times when I could work on my treehouse. As I said, I wasn't much of a rule follower, and I figured that as long as we were within sight of my older sister, who was in charge when my parents were away, we'd be fine.

So, we began building our own amazing treehouse one Saturday morning, right after my parents left to work on the duplex. I gathered some boards that I'd found that would work great for the base of the treehouse. We were planning to nail four of these together in a square attached to four trees that seemed perfectly situated for the treehouse.

Nailing these four boards to support the treehouse took longer than I expected. When things took longer than I wanted them to take, my mind would often wander to the next adventure, which is what happened after we'd been working for a few hours. We'd just finished putting up three of the four boards for the perimeter of the treehouse. I was very excited to finally get the third board up, and I wanted to check to see how stable they were. So, I climbed up on one of them and stood on it. It seemed firm enough, and I told my younger brother that I wanted to test the board across from me. He said he'd move the ladder so I could climb down then go back up to test the other board.

For any young boy, moving the ladder would be way too time-consuming. Instead, I held onto a branch and began to swing hard toward the other board we'd nailed up. In my mind, this was a simple leap from the branch to the board. All I had to do was swing hard enough, let go at the right time, and then catch the other board I was swinging toward.

What a young boy thinks will happen doesn't always work out like he'd planned. When I swung out, I let go of the branch and missed the board by about two feet. I slammed hard into the ground, and I heard and felt a snap in my left arm. Yes, I had broken my arm.

Immediately my younger brother ran to tell our older sister. She scolded me for leaving the fenced area, then went inside and called our mom to come get me and take me to the hospital. For the rest of the summer, I wore a cast and missed so many other fun adventures.

Later in life, I thought about that incident and what lessons I could learn from it. The first lesson could be, *Don't put yourself in a position that you aren't supposed to be in the first place.* Like me and my brother being outside the fence. Or maybe, *Think about the consequences of letting go and all that it will entail.* Or even, *Just use the ladder; it's easier.*

But what I learned most that day was this: Letting go lets you live the life you always dreamed of living. You'll never know if you're going to make it until you're willing to let go and take flight. If you're truly going to live the life you always wanted to live, you need to reduce your fear of letting go to the point that your faith in God is greater than any fear of what's out there. And even if you don't make it, and it doesn't turn out like you'd hoped, God still has you.

> *You'll never know if you're going to make it until you're willing to let go and take flight.*

I can tell you that at fifty years old, my arm has healed just fine. I'm sure that if they took an X-ray, they'd find a scar from when I broke my arm, but I've recovered very well. Scars just leave the stories of the life we've lived. I have a lot of scars, but I also have a great story—and lesson—from the day I decided to let go and trust that I might just make it.

From the beginning of creation, we were designed with eternity in mind. We were meant to let go of those things that are temporal and reach for those things that will last for eternity. God wants us to hold on to things loosely in our lives. We are to let go and, by faith, reach for the life that God designed for us to live.

I wrote this book because I've learned since a young boy and now as an adult that we cannot live the life we want to live until we're willing to let go of what we know we should release. We need to trust that God has something good for us. Many times, we grip so hard to where we are that we cannot get to where God is trying to move us. I encourage you to relax and loosen your grip, then you will actually be able to let go.

As you read my stories about the tough decisions I've had to make to let go of some pretty important things and ideas, I hope they inspire you to do the same—to let go of those things you want and need to let go of, so you can live the life God has planned for you.

1

I'M AFRAID I'LL MAKE THE WRONG DECISION!

When I was a junior in high school, I carpooled back and forth to school with my friend, Mike Young. His father was a salesman for a major company in the Saint Louis area, and he flew all over the United States selling their products. Mr. Young often picked us up, and during those rides home, he told us incredible stories about his travels. He talked about all the cool cities he visited and the planes he took to get there. It sounded like the most amazing job, and I knew I wanted to be like Mike's dad and travel worldwide, working in sales.

I graduated high school in 1989, and that same year, I started working for my father in the distribution company my parents had purchased in 1980. They'd bought the company in hopes that one day it would supply enough income for them to fund their desire to be full-time missionaries. When I joined, my father had just transitioned the company from a distribution company to a pet shampoo company.

Our company rented shampoo systems to dog groomers. The shampoo systems included an air compressor, a five-gallon tank for holding liquid dog shampoo, and a spray applicator. My father and my brother, Don, were the only full-time employees, and they went to pet grooming salons and installed our equipment in salons all over the United States. If a system ever needed repair, we either sent the customer the repair part or went to fix it for them.

Although I had no desire to go to college, I had no idea what I wanted to do with my life. I only knew that I wanted nothing more to do with formal education. And I felt the pressure to choose the right course in life. At seventeen, I felt like I was expected to make decisions that would affect the rest of my life.

The week after I graduated, my father took me on a road trip to install and service these shampoo systems. We traveled from Saint Louis, Missouri, to Miami, Florida, and installed eleven shampoo systems that week. The company wasn't making a lot of money yet, so we couldn't afford to sleep in hotels. Instead, we slept in our small minivan. We parked and slept in either a hotel parking lot or a rest area alongside the highway.

Before this trip, I'd never traveled further east than Illinois. But now I saw parts of the country I'd only heard about. I knew this was what I wanted to do with my life. I began thinking, *If I can convince Dad to let me go out and do this on my own, I'll be able to travel all over the country, be on my own, and do what I want to do.*

That week, however, didn't turn out as pleasant and glorious as I thought it was going to be. I was a seventeen-year-old young man wanting to prove my way in life, and my father was a man who was under a lot of pressure to make the company profitable and stay in business—not to mention that we were cramped together and sleeping in a small minivan. We couldn't get away from each other, and it wasn't a good week for relationship building. It was quite a frustrating trip for both my father and me.

From the beginning, we got on each other's nerves. It got so bad that, at one point, I didn't speak to my father unless I absolutely had to. He'd gotten upset with me for something I didn't do, and I thought he owed me an apology. In my mind, he'd wronged me. I thought, *I'm not going to speak to him until he makes it right with me.*

Fortunately for me, Dad was a bigger man than me, and on the twenty-hour drive home from Orlando, he apologized. This opened up the conversation, and we talked about my role in the company.

"I want to travel on my own and sell for the company without any more guidance. I know I can do this, but I need to do it on my own," I said.

My dad listened to me and said, "I believe you were meant to be in sales, and you'll make a good salesman. I'll pay you $600 a month to travel and install the shampoo systems if that's what you really want to do."

I couldn't believe it. My dreams were coming true. I'd barely made it through high school with a GPA of 2.3, and now I'd be traveling on my own around the country.

Two weeks later, I packed up my father's 1983 Chevrolet Caprice Classic. I put as many shampoo systems and gallons of shampoo as I could fit in that car and headed out to begin my career as a salesman in the pet industry. I left that Sunday after church, and that week, I drove over three thousand miles. I began my week in upper New York state, drove down through New Jersey, Virginia, North Carolina, and ended up in Atlanta, Georgia, before heading home on Saturday afternoon. During my travels, I'd outsold both my brother's and father's best weeks of selling gallons of shampoo as an add-on sale to the shampoo system installations. My future was now secure, and I'd spend the next twenty-nine years trying to top every sale the company had previously made.

During those years, we developed many different brands of products that are now sold both domestically and internationally. I opened new areas of distribution for the company, and we went from selling directly to the pet salon owner to selling through distributors that sold to pet store retailers, large multichain companies, and private label products for companies like Nestle Purina and Disney. We also launched the product brands internationally to over seventy-two countries.

I could never have dreamed I'd be a part of all of this, nor would I understand that one day I'd have to give it all up right when I was at the pinnacle of success. God had given me this desire of my heart, yet at the same time, He would move me to give it all up when the company was becoming a powerful brand in the pet industry around the world.

Letting Go

Just three years after I started working, my other brothers, Darin and Denver, also joined the company. Now my father,

Don Sr., was building Cosmos Corporation with his four sons. Fortunately, we didn't need many more employees. We had one other employee named Marie, who was sixty-seven years old. Marie taught us how to make liquid shampoo products.

My parents had always wanted to be missionaries who preached the gospel and helped the poor and needy in third-world countries. So, in 1992, when Hurricane Andrew with its category-5 winds hit the coast of Florida, they felt called to go help with the relief effort. They left in mid-September and spent the next nine months helping the people of Miami-Dade rebuild after the devastation left by this hurricane. Of course, the profits from the company supported them during this work, which put them in touch with other organizations and churches, both domestically and internationally. One of those organizations had sent thirty people from Guatemala on a bus to Miami. My parents learned about the group from one of the local Miami churches and contacted their leader. With my parents' help, the Guatemalans found a large, open field where they would live in tents for the next nine months while they helped people clean up and get back to some sense of normalcy after the devastating hurricane.

That time in Miami solidified my parents' desire to become full-time missionaries. So, in 1994, they invited my brothers and me to become partial owners of the company. Over the next twenty-seven years, they traveled all over the world and brought the gospel and aid to areas of the world that were desperate for both spiritual and physical help.

As their work continued, they launched an organization called Gifts of Love International for this purpose. In 2006, they bought a twenty-two-acre piece of property next to a river in the countryside of Guatemala and established a forever children's home for severely abused children. When they opened their first home on the property in 2012, they received their first child—a baby who'd been abandoned by her birth mother. Over the next eight years, they'd see hundreds of children come through this home.

Eventually, my parents started to get older and couldn't do all the things they'd once done. At the same time, my brothers and I felt called to step into the next season of our lives and continue what my parents had started through their missionary work. Yet, at the same time, we had a company to run that provided the money for my parents' mission work. We were all involved—even consumed—with the company and its day-to-day leadership. Then a great tragedy began the process of moving each of us out of our roles in the company, whether we wanted to or not.

On March 11, 2014, our lives and our company would change forever. Matt Adam, my best friend since I was six years old and my brother Darin's brother-in-law for the past twenty-five years, was riding his motorcycle to work at our company. On the way, he met up with my niece's fiancé, Jake Boedeker, and his best friend, Adam Meyer, who were also riding their motorcycles to work for us that day. They just happened to meet up at an intersection and decided to follow each other for the remaining two miles. But they never made it. A school bus hesitated at a stop sign, and Matt, who was the lead rider, hit the front of the bus. Jake hit the back tire while Adam laid his motorcycle down and slid under the back of the bus. Both Matt, forty-two, and Jake, twenty-two, were killed instantly.

How can words describe what each of these men meant to so many? Over 1,500 people attended each of their funerals. The impact of their deaths would ripple through our company and our family for many years to come. Though we didn't see it at the time, after their deaths, we began questioning what we truly wanted or what we were supposed to do with our lives. Were we meant only to build a company that supported other works in the world? Or was there something more that each of us was to do outside of the company's walls?

This tragedy began to move my brothers and me into the next phase of what God had in store for us. The Bible says that what Satan meant for harm, God meant for the good of those who love Him. I believe that the hurts and pain this tragic accident brought about began a shift in each of our minds and hearts. I began to feel the tension between each of us and our desire to do more for those that we were given responsibility for outside the walls of our company.

A few years later, I began to sense that God was calling each of us away from our positions in the company and into a new role in our lives. I told Laura that I was ready to make a change and move other people into my position. In fact, I told her the same thing so many times during 2016 and 2017 that she got frustrated that I didn't ever let go and do something about it.

"I just want to quit and have someone else run this company," I said for the umpteenth time while standing in our kitchen one evening.

Laura and I had been arguing a lot lately, and her response was curt. "Fine," she replied. "Either do it or stop talking about it. I'm tired of hearing you say it without doing anything about it."

I was taken aback by her response, yet at the same time, I was enormously afraid to let go of what I'd built (at least my end of the company). I felt like I was the only person who could fulfill my position.

One day, I felt God speak to me. I heard Him say that in the same way that He would used each of us to grow the company, if we would release our positions and step into the work my parents had done, we'd see massive growth in the company *and* in the ministry.

I knew I'd heard from God, and I even told my brothers about it. But how would this even be possible? Each of us had such an intricate role in the company. We were the initiators, innovators, leaders, and decision makers. Our teams relied and depended upon us for so many aspects of our roles. If each of us stepped out of our role, how would the company ever make it?

If We Don't Let Go, God Will Move Us to That Change

In the summer of 2017, Andy, an employee I totally trusted, came to speak with me about a decision he needed to make regarding one of our customers. During that time, I told him about a call I'd gotten from Bill, one of our leaders, who was at a trade show with another sales rep. Andy asked me whether he should travel to see the customer in question.

I said to Andy, "Bill's at a trade show with another rep. I just spoke with him, and he's going to call me when he has a free moment. I'll ask for his opinion when he calls."

At this, Andy had a very inquisitive look on his face but said nothing.

When Bill called, I asked him how the trade show was going.

"It was a little slow but is beginning to pick up," he said. "I have a meeting in a few hours with the owner of the company. I'll speak to him about the upcoming promotion we're doing."

I asked Bill about Andy's request, and Bill gave his input for making the decision. I didn't suspect that anything was out of place.

Later that day, Andy came to my office again and said, "Where's Bill?"

"He's at the trade show," I answered. "Why are you asking?"

"I was just wondering because I thought Bill was somewhere else this week. I must have been mistaken." We talked a little longer, and Andy left my office and never brought it up again.

A month later, my brothers and I had a meeting with a consultant, Mark Bartig, and for six hours, we talked to him about how we could move our company forward while possibly stepping out of our leadership positions. We each felt we were meant to begin new chapters in our lives, but we all felt obligated to our current roles in the company. We thought things like, *We built this company over the last twenty-five years; how could there be another person who could replace us and do what we do?*

Other companies had expressed interest in buying us, but we knew that if we sold the company, we'd never see the reward of the growth potential for the company. So, we'd invited Mark in to talk with us about our desires for the company. He was very familiar with our challenges because he worked for an investment firm that bought and sold companies like ours.

We asked Mark a simple question.

"If your company bought us and put you in charge of exponential growth, what would you do as the leader to make this happen?"

Mark said, "I'd go out and hire the best CEO, CFO, HR Director, and VP of Sales that I could find. I would impress upon them the desires I had for the company, and then I'd step out of the way and let them do what they were hired to do."

Mark suggested that we had two options. "You could sell the company, take the money, and go do what you want to do, or you could take the longer and harder road and do what I suggested and hire good leaders to run the company."

After Mark left the meeting, my brothers and I stayed to discuss all we'd heard. We felt that the right decision was to keep going the way we were, and if we could figure out who could fill these strategic positions, we would do that over time. Fortunately for us, the Bible says in Proverbs, "A man makes his plan, but God determines his steps." And though we didn't know it that day, God would have us stepping out of our roles faster than we expected.

After that meeting, I boarded a plane for Brazil to spend a week with one of our major distributors. I arrived early the next morning, and our distributor picked me up from the airport. I began my week of meetings with both their related partners and some of their other customers. Three days later, my brother Darin called me just as we were sitting down to an authentic Brazilian steak-house lunch with a customer.

"Derrik, do you have time to talk with me and a group of people?" Darin asked. "I need to speak with you about a situation."

"I just sat down to have lunch with a very important account," I said. "Could we do this later?"

"We can, but I need you to call us at 5:00 p.m. It's very serious."

I went back to the lunch meeting and told our distributor and the client, "I have a very important meeting at 5:00 p.m. Could I please be back at my hotel by then for this call?"

I got on the Skype call at 5:00. To my astonishment, my three brothers and four other employees, including Andy, were on the call. Andy led the meeting, and he told me that Bill had lied to me. The day Bill had said that he was with one of our major distributors, he was actually in another city. He spoke of Bill's deception and the many times he had misrepresented his travel over the past few years. Andy had valid proof to back up his claims. I was dumbfounded that he could have pulled off this deception for so long.

Since we'd met Mark a week earlier and he had suggested that we find someone to replace each of us, I'd been thinking of who might take over for my position—and I naturally thought of Bill. I thought he'd do a great job. I had no clue how God was protecting us from making a very serious wrong decision.

Of course, we had to terminate Bill, and to this day, it was one of the hardest struggles in my corporate life. After Bill left,

I heard story after story from employees who'd been deceived and manipulated by Bill for years.

At the end of this long, hard week, I was in my office around 2:00 p.m. when another employee asked to see me. He told me of other things I hadn't known and asked me for help. By the time the meeting was over, it was 3:30. I was completely exhausted from all that had gone on that week, and when my wife called me around 4:00 and asked, "How are you doing?" I broke down and cried for the next few minutes.

"Do you want to come to the Homecoming football game tonight?" she asked. "Raquel's performing."

"Yes, I plan to be there. I just need some time alone to be with God first."

I spent a little over an hour thanking God for His wisdom and guidance that week, and soon I felt my strength coming back. That evening I went to the football game and really enjoyed being there. I was so grateful for God's hand of protection on our lives and our company and for leading us through the steps of our lives.

The following week, I planned to meet with my friend Guy. Guy had said that the company for which he was a vice president had made changes, and he didn't know how to proceed. I wanted to know what he was going through and to see if I could offer any advice. Through this conversation, I wondered, *Could Guy become our VP of Sales and replace me?*

I quickly called my brother, Darin, and mentioned my idea to him.

"Wait," Darin said. "A half hour ago, I was thinking about Guy, and I texted him to see how he was doing. Then I started thinking that Guy might be interested in *my* job—the VP of Marketing!"

That Darin and I both thought of Guy for a VP position in our company could only be God.

"We probably couldn't afford him," Darin added. "He's been the VP of a major corporation, and we don't have those kind of dollars to offer."

"Maybe not," I said. "But we should at least speak to him."

By the end of October, we'd come to an agreement for Guy to become the Vice President of Sales and Marketing for Cosmos Corporation, thus replacing both Darin and me. However, one problem remained.

Guy asked, "Who do I report to?"

My brother Don filled both the CEO and CFO roles, but he was also thinking about his exit.

"We're working through this and will get back to you on that."

Earlier that year, we'd promoted Don's son-in-law, Landon Hobson, to be Director of Operations. Landon did an amazing job and had won the hearts of all those who worked for him. He was an incredible leader and came to his position with three master's degrees: a Master of Arts in Christian Thought, a Master's in Leadership and Development, and a Master's in International Economics. He was definitely qualified to be the CEO of our company, both in education and in function.

We also needed someone who could work closely with Landon and was qualified in finance. Don's son, Bradley, had worked with our company for years and had started his education in finance the year before. Though he didn't yet have a degree, he was determined to do all he could to make our company a success.

In 2017, during the Thanksgiving lunch we hosted for the company, we announced both Landon as the CEO of Cosmos Corporation and Bradley as the Director of Finance. Now we had the two people in place who could take the company forward. Guy would start on December 1 as the VP of Sales and Marketing, reporting directly to Landon, our new CEO.

Guy needed a place to work, so I gave up my office and had a new office constructed from the smaller coffee room that would be right next to his office. I asked my daughter, Raquel, to decorate it for me, and with her artistic touches, I came to love my new workspace. Even though I had to let go of the office I'd enjoyed for years, there was something exciting about letting go of one area of my life so someone else could become a success in a new area of their life.

I wish I could say that the changes were an easy transition and that everything was rosy from there on out. However, the next year was one of the hardest and most challenging of my life.

In September 2017, I'd just completed the largest one-time sale our company had ever closed, and I'd landed one of the largest accounts for our company. Both were significant accomplishments for me, and now I was turning over all domestic sales to someone new to the industry—one I'd been proficient in for the past twenty-eight years. It was very hard for me to hand over the relationships I'd built, and I didn't feel like I was an important part of the transition. Instead, I felt like I'd been replaced. I felt left out of many of the transition points and decisions.

For the next six months, I continued as the Vice President of International Sales, and I had oversight of that last large account we'd landed back in September. I tried as much as I could to keep up with all the changes in leadership, as well as not get in the way of what Guy was doing with domestic sales and as the VP of Marketing—but it was hard. I realized that if I stayed in my current position, it would cause confusion and frustration within our team. So in March of 2018, I sat down with Landon and told him that I thought Guy should assume responsibility for all sales of the company by June—about one year earlier than we had planned.

Over the next couple of months, I turned over my responsibilities to Guy, and we looked for my replacement to take care of the large customer I was still overseeing. On June 1, Landon said they'd conducted a lot of interviews and had found the person to take over the account. She had extensive knowledge of working with large companies, as well as an e-commerce background. She was exactly who we needed.

I asked Landon, "Will she work out of a cubicle or an office?"

"I'd love to give her an office, but we don't have any left," he said.

I thought about it for a moment, then said, "She can have my office. It doesn't make sense for me to have an office when I travel like I do. She should have mine."

"No," Landon said. "You're an owner of the company, and you should have an office."

"I'll only offer it to you this last time. If you say no, I won't offer it again."

He laughed and said, "OK. Thank you. I'll let her know you gave it up for her."

It was no longer a theory or a future idea. I was now *letting go* of the only role I'd known since I was seventeen years old.

On the morning of June 19, I boxed up everything my daughter Raquel had brought to decorate my office. I gathered all the papers that were important to me and everything that represented what I'd accomplished over the last twenty-nine years, including a picture of Jake and Matt. It all fit in five boxes. Then I began to cry. I thought to myself, *I'm giving up everything. What am I doing? What if this is the wrong decision? Why am I having to do this all on my own?*

> *It was no longer a theory or a future idea. I was now letting go of the only role I'd known since I was seventeen years old.*

I was all alone as I wrapped up my career. I carried those five boxes out of our building, and no one asked if they could help me. My mind raced. *Yes, this is good for everyone else, but what about me? Have I made the right decision to give up my career, my role in our company? Have I made the right decision to give up my office? Am I doing the right thing?*"

I didn't get very far down the street when all the emotions hit me again, and I pulled over and wept. Out of great fear, I questioned myself. *Did I make a mistake?*

When we reach a crossroads in life, we're often afraid of making the wrong decision. But unless we can release the grip on that thing we want the most, we may never achieve what we were meant to achieve. We're in danger of being choked by fear that we'll make the wrong decision, and we may lose out on discovering what we could do to fulfill our calling.

Now, many years later, I can tell you that letting go of my position and office was one of the best decisions for my life, as well as for our company. It catapulted my wife and me into new areas where we needed to grow. It empowered others to make the decisions they needed to make, and it allowed them to take the reins of the company and grow it into the next phase. Neither my brothers nor I could have accomplished this growth because we didn't have the gifts and talents that our new leadership team had.

There's a story that Jesus told about how we must learn to live our lives if we want to grow. John 12:20–26 (NKJV) reads:

Now there were certain Greeks among those who came up to worship at the feast. Then they came to Philip, who was from Bethsaida of Galilee, and asked him, saying, "Sir, we wish to see Jesus." Philip came and told Andrew, and in turn Andrew and Philip told Jesus.

But Jesus answered them, saying, "The hour has come that the Son of Man should be glorified. Most assuredly, I say to you, ***unless a grain of wheat falls into the ground and dies, it remains alone; but if it dies, it produces much grain. He who loves his life will lose it, and he who hates his life in this world will keep it for eternal life.*** *If anyone serves Me, let him follow Me; and where I am, there My servant will be also. If anyone serves Me, him My Father will honor.*

A plant reproduces itself when the fruit from that plant falls off and dies. When the seed that's inside the fruit is replanted, it can produce ten, one hundred, even one thousand times itself. If you look inside an apple, you'll see that it has many seeds. If you took those apple seeds and replanted them, those seeds could produce another apple tree that would produce apples for many years to come.

I know this sounds silly, but what if the apple said to the branch that was holding it,

"I don't want to let go. It's going to hurt when I hit the ground, and I'll get bruised and broken."

The branch says to the apple, "I know you're afraid, but unless you let go, you'll never become the beautiful apple tree you were born to be."

The apple replies, "I'm afraid to let go. What if I let go, fall to the ground, and get smashed?"

"Unless you let go and are smashed, you'll never become the tree you're meant to be," says the branch.

We can come up with all kinds of excuses when we're afraid to let go of that which is holding us back from the growth we were meant to enjoy. Yet it isn't until we let go and let that thing die that we wanted the most that we can produce the growth and fruit we were meant to produce.

In this parable, Jesus is trying to explain that loving your life because of what you have now or concentrating on your own success will keep you from the destiny you were created to reach. He is speaking of things that are much greater than letting go of a position in a company or an office. He is speaking about those who aren't willing to let go of this physical life for a spiritual life that will endure for eternity.

If you aren't willing to die to your desires or what you are holding on to the tightest—like I was with my position in the company—how can you be stretched into producing more of what God has for you? We mustn't be afraid to make the decisions to let go of what we hold dear in order to reach that to which Christ is calling us.

If you aren't willing to die to your desires or what you are holding on to the tightest—like I was with my position in the company—how can you be stretched into producing more of what God has for you?

Here are some practical ways to learn to let go of your fear of making a wrong decision:

- **Just step out!** Once you choose to step into that decision, you'll begin to put things in motion that bring that decision to life. Often, the way to get to the destination you want to reach is to take the first step. Decide to *step out* in faith. That's what I had to do when I decided to give up my position, so our company could have peace, and I wouldn't be an obstacle to the growth we were sure to have.

- **Nothing will change until you make a decision, so decide to make that decision!** Once you've made the decision to step out, you'll see a result. There's no wrong decision because your decisions become part of learning experiences. Our lives are filled with numerous learning experiences that come from the decisions we've made in the past. And if you aren't satisfied with the decision you make, you can always make another decision. To get rid of the fear of making the wrong decision, *decide to make the decision.* For years, I knew that we needed to make a change in leadership, but it wasn't until *we decided to make the decision* that we could put the things in place to have the new leadership we needed.

- **Be intentional in your decision!** When you're intentional about your decision, the fear that you may be wrong disappears. If I hadn't been intentional in giving up my office to Landon, I might have never been drawn into that next area of life where God was taking me.

Fear has been described as *False Evidence Appearing Real.* Let that fear inside you die and plant a new seed of faith. Learn to let go and see what God will do. I can promise you this: Letting go will probably be one of the hardest and, at the same time, most rewarding decisions you will ever make.

2

HOW CAN I KNOW IF I HEARD FROM GOD?

When our oldest daughter was just three or four years old, Laura and I decided to move from the subdivision where we'd been living and build a new house in the country. I'd grown up with horses and had always wanted my kids to have that experience too. So, we started looking for a piece of land and researching what kind of house we'd build on it.

Even as we began this process, we could feel God leading us to an amazing dream property that overlooked a valley. I still remember the day we found it on Easter of 2002. It was so amazing; to the west, you could see for ten miles, and to the east, it overlooked the Mississippi River into Illinois. We could build our house on top of the hill, the front facing east and overlooking the Mississippi River flatlands where we could watch the sunrise, the back facing west over the large valley for some amazing sunsets.

That day I began to dream about the house with a barn at the bottom of the hill behind it. I pictured the fenced-off pasture, the horses in the field, and our family enjoying the day with them. Though we fell in love with this property, there was a catch. The seller didn't want to close on the deal until he found another property to reinvest his money.

Later that evening, we tendered an offer to purchase the property, accepting the fact that we'd have to wait to close until the seller found something else. We didn't know how long this would take but later realized it was a blessing because we didn't have to make any payments on this property for over a year. Even in this, God was showing us His favor for us to own the property.

During that year, Laura and I looked at many different plans for houses we could build. We viewed hundreds of blueprints but could never settle on one that was exactly right for us. At times, it was frustrating because we couldn't agree on a house that would work for both of us, mainly because I was impatient and wanted to move forward with the build. Even so, there was one set of plans that stood out to us that we kept coming back to. We both loved everything about the layout and look of the house, but the price tag for building it was way out of our budget.

One evening, I was sitting on the couch and staring at these plans when suddenly, I felt that God was revealing them to me in a new way. I began to see that if we made some changes to the drawings and delayed building out some of the areas—like the basement and attic space—we could afford to build this beautiful house. I also realized that if we used builder-grade products for now, we could upgrade the house in future years with the materials we wanted, like quartz countertops, hardwood floors throughout the house, and stone to cover the back of the house like the plans showed.

I told Laura, "I think I figured out a way we can build this house."

As I began to tell her about the adjustments, we began to get excited. I still remember Laura saying, "I can't believe we may actually be able to build this house. It just took us a while to see it."

I think God opened my eyes to see the plans in a new way. I believe He was speaking to me, and He allowed me to see the plans from His perspective. And during our time of extended research, I think God was teaching us to listen to Him and be patient for what He had for us. As I've learned to listen to Him, I believe there are many ways that God guides us (speaks to us), and that evening was one of those times.

Now that we had a concept for our house, we needed an architect to draw up the detailed plans. We hired someone who'd recently opened his company and was looking for new clients. We explained that what we loved most about this house was the view we'd have from the back as we drove up the road to the house. We wanted to preserve how the back of the house looked on the plans and wanted to design the house from the back to the front. I listened to everything that Laura loved most about the house and made sure the architect designed it that way. We were ready to build as soon as we sealed the deal on the property.

I decided to be the general contractor on the build and began to get bids from subcontractors. During this same time, Laura was pregnant with our second daughter, who was born in November 2003. Having a new baby, picking out everything we wanted in our house, building the house, and running a multimillion-dollar sales team was not the easiest thing to do. I really don't know how we were able to multitask so many things, but a short six months later, we'd built our 4,500-square-foot dream home. We moved in on September 30, 2004.

About a month after we moved in, I was exhausted, but we still had so much that needed to be done. We'd spent the last two years designing and building this house, and I was ready to start enjoying the amazing home that God had provided. One night as the sun was setting behind the house, I walked across the road and sat down to look at our home. I really loved what Laura and I had built together and was amazed at what we'd been able to do in such a short period.

I could see into the window of the dining room and watched as our oldest daughter walked her little sister into the empty room to play. My heart filled, and I began to cry. I asked God, "Why have You been so good to me?"

I felt God answer, "I will use this house as a testimony in this community of a family who truly loves Me."

I'm always amazed by how God uses the simplest things in life to show me how much He desires to have a relationship with me. It's another way that God speaks to me, through the thoughts He reveals to me in my own mind.

Our daughter Raquel celebrated her first birthday a month after we moved in. We invited our entire family to come over, even though we didn't have much furniture. It was a special time to celebrate a new chapter in our family. We had so much fun showing everyone the house and letting Raquel enjoy the first of over sixteen birthdays celebrated there.

Her first major gift from us was a little play set that had a door with a doorbell. When we rang the doorbell, she crawled through the door and then played with a couple fun toys that were on the other side. Looking back, I believe that play set was symbolic of God telling us to go through the door and see what He had on the other side.

Winter came and went, and spring was right around the corner. In late February, I started making plans to build a barn and to plan out the pasture for the two horses we'd just bought. I was still traveling a lot for my job, so I wanted to make the care of the horses as easy as possible for Laura while I was gone. The house was on top of the hill overlooking the property below, and I wanted to keep as much open pasture as possible, so we wouldn't have to buy much hay during the winter. The right side of our property was all woods. The best place for the barn was at the bottom of the hill, situated within the woods. I could remove a group of trees and build the barn and riding corral where these trees originally stood. Over the next three months, I hired different companies to install a driveway to the barn, build the barn, and install a three-rail white vinyl fence that enclosed three acres of the property.

One Saturday morning, I picked up the horses, Sugar and Peaches, and brought them out in the field as a surprise for the girls. They were so excited when they saw the horses in the field. That afternoon we had fun hanging out and playing with the horses.

We ended up selling both these horses and went through a few different ones until we finally settled on four different horses that fit each one of us. It was a dream fulfilled that God had put in my heart.

We also ended up with three miniature horses that were all part of the same family. The first was Cotton. Cotton had a baby that we named Candy, and Candy had a baby we called Apple. Both Elise and Raquel learned to ride on the miniatures before moving up to the bigger horses. We eventually gave up Cotton and Candy to other owners and kept Apple for ourselves.

It had always been my dream to have the girls ride alongside me as we went on adventure rides on our horses. We eventually bought a large horse trailer and spent many weekends going to a local horse park and riding the trails together. It was a great time to talk and understand what was going on in each girl's life.

I believe that God gives us the dreams of our hearts, meaning that He places these dreams inside of us, and it's up to us to fulfill these dreams. These dreams are God speaking to us.

When we'd first designed our house, we thought that about five years in, we'd start the upgrades. Our five-year plan turned into twelve years. When I started making more money in my job, we thought about the things we wanted to do to the house. First on the list was to upgrade its exterior look.

In March of 2011, we started removing all the vinyl siding to replace it with cement board siding. We added stone to the back of the house to give it the look we'd seen in the original plans. We also had a custom-built waterproof floor put on the second-floor deck. Now we could be outside on rainy days. This project took the better part of 2011, and it was finished in the fall of that year.

In the summer of 2012, we hired a pool company to dig out our backyard and install a custom in-ground pool. We had all the bells and whistles added to this pool, including a rock waterfall that emptied back into the pool. Building the pool required us to have multiple block-retaining walls built, which pushed the entire project into the spring of 2013. The project was finished by the end of March 2013, and we had our first pool party for Elise's birthday that April.

After we finished the pool, it was time to finish the basement. In June of 2014, we hired a company to begin this project. This time, we hired an interior designer to help Laura with all the details. This project went on for the better part of 2014, and we finally completed it in time for Christmas. We loved the open area for playing games. We installed a large-screen television with theatre-style seating, which became a favorite place for us to hang out as a family and watch movies together.

Just when we thought we had the house how we wanted it, Laura and I began talking about refreshing the interior of the house. In the spring of 2016, we hired an interior designer to help us with some minor upgrades like painting the walls, some new flooring, and a few updates to the kitchen. As with many projects, this one grew—and grew. Over the next eighteen months, we totally redid the kitchen, removed all the carpeting and installed vinyl plank wood flooring, replaced the fireplace, totally redid the laundry room, added crown molding to all the main areas of the house, and repainted all the walls and doors.

We finished updating all the rooms (except the master bedroom and bathroom) just in time for Elise to graduate from high school in April of 2017. It was so nice to have all these things completed to make that day special and allow her to have a nice time at her party.

After that, we decided to finish the master bedroom and bath with the upgrades we wanted. This shouldn't have taken very long—about three to four weeks. However, it turned into four months because of all the extra things we elected to do, like extra crown molding, heated bathroom floors, and an entire custom closet. By the spring of 2018, we'd completed everything we ever thought we'd want in our dream home and planned to live here for the rest of our lives.

However, a very small event happened in the fall of 2017 that made me start to question if this house was really our forever home. In September of 2017, I took the horses to an Amish farrier to have the horse's hooves trimmed and horseshoes reset. When I was on my way back home, I started thinking about the upcoming master bedroom project when this question came to my mind: *How much does the house actually matter to me?* About three miles from the house, I could see it from a distance. I noticed that I wasn't as attached to it as I once had been. It was a very odd feeling for me because we'd put so much effort into making it our dream property. I thought to myself, *Maybe I'm losing it. I better see what Laura thinks.*

When I got home, I made a cup of coffee and leaned against the new countertops that had been installed the previous spring. Laura was standing in her new dream kitchen, and we talked about the day.

"You know," I said, "we just spent the last five years making this house everything we ever dreamed of, but I don't know that I feel attached to it anymore."

I waited for Laura to tell me that I was crazy and what did we just spend these last five years doing all this for. We'd been fighting a lot lately, and I was certain I'd just opened a can of worms that would lead to another argument. But that's not what happened.

"I know what you mean," she answered. "I've been feeling the same way."

I thought to myself, *WHAT?* Laura had just spent the last three years with an interior designer picking out everything that would make this place ours. *She put so much effort into the redesign of the house, and now she doesn't feel attached either. How is this even possible?*

We talked about it for a while and decided to give it some time and pray about what we were feeling. I can't say that we spent the next two years in deep prayer over this, but the more we talked about it, the more we felt that we wouldn't be in the house for the rest of our lives. But at the same time, we didn't feel like God was leading us to sell.

Over the next couple years, as Elise moved on to college and Raquel began to get more involved with everything she had going on, we didn't get as much time with the horses, and they became more of a chore than an enjoyment for me. In the spring of 2019, it was time to let others enjoy what we'd once loved so much. We researched good homes for the horses, and by July, we'd found each of them new homes with families that would love them as much as we had.

Meanwhile, earlier that May, my friend, John, had asked if he could come ride the horses with me. I told him that we'd better hurry up because we were selling them soon. As we rode the horses, we talked about life and the many changes we were both going through.

As we rode, I could see our house off in the distance. John owned seventeen rental properties, and he frequently bought and sold houses, so I asked, "Is now a good time to sell a house?"

"It's not a bad time," he said, "and you never know what next year will bring." Of course, no one knew that the following February would bring COVID-19.

"For a couple years, Laura and I have been contemplating whether we should sell," I said. "But we don't know that we've heard God say, 'Thus saith moveth.'"

John's answer was thoughtful. "Sometimes God speaks to us by taking our previous desires away, and He wants us to move by faith when we have a thought to do something."

"Sometimes God speaks to us by taking our previous desires away, and He wants us to move by faith when we have a thought to do something."

Those words set a course that would significantly change our lives forever.

After our ride, John left, and I went up to the house. Laura was working in the kitchen, and I told her what John had said about selling the house. We discussed it for about an hour, then decided that we'd step out in faith and see what God would do.

The next day I started searching for a real estate agent who could sell our house and help us find a piece of property where we could build something new. It was amazing to see how everything came together over the next few days. Yet I was still questioning if we'd actually heard from God or if we were acting on our emotions.

We were referred to a real estate agent, and we immediately knew that her firm would be the perfect group to represent us. I began searching for the plans to a house that Laura and I had visited in California a couple of years earlier. We'd known at the time that we'd love to retire in a house very similar to it. As I searched, I found the layout of that exact house. Now we could hire an architect to draw the plans for our next house. That same weekend, we went to look at a property that was high on a cliff and overlooked the Missouri River Bottoms. It was an absolutely beautiful view, but because of the drop-off of the property, the house that we wanted to build would not fit. But as we were pulling out of the subdivision, Laura noticed a lot that backed up to some woods where the house might fit. However, it didn't have the view that we wanted.

The next day I went back to see if the house would work on the lot. The more I walked the property and plotted out the house, the more excited I got that this might be the place. I called Laura and began laughing because I was so excited. We were sold.

Within five days, we'd selected a real estate agent, found the layout for our new home, and decided on the property where we would build it. No, we didn't hear the audible voice of God telling us to do any of these things, but it was amazing to see how everything came together so quickly. We knew it had to be God speaking to us in this way.

Over the next couple weeks, we cleaned our house and did the fixes our agent had suggested we do before putting the house on the market. I still felt like we were in the will of God, but I kept wondering if I'd actually heard from God on this. As I read my Bible, I asked God if we should sell the house or not.

One July morning, as I was praying, in a quiet whisper in my mind, I heard, "It is not wrong or right for you to sell the house. Just be patient."

I knew this had to be God because the last thing I was at that time in my life was patient.

I still felt like we were in the will of God, but I kept wondering if I'd actually heard from God on this.

So, we listed the house—a huge step of faith—because it set a course for changes from which we couldn't turn back. We would be letting go of all the dreams we'd once had for our life in this house. Though we'd felt God's presence in all the steps leading up to this, I still feared that I hadn't actually heard God tell me to *let go* of the house. But we stepped out in faith and set the next course of our lives in motion, trusting that God would determine our steps.

God never said, "Thus saith moveth," but I'm not sure that's actually how God always speaks to us. Because I grew up in a church that shared about hearing God speak to the individual, that was my expectation. Now we were simply moving in faith and waiting to see what God would do.

Days turned into weeks, and weeks turned into months with no buyer. I kept telling myself, *God may not have said to sell the house, but He did say, "Be patient."* Our six-month contract with our real estate agent was coming to an end. Questions arose that needed answers, such as whether we should extend another six months, choose another agent, or take the house off the market altogether. Then God spoke to Laura through something at church one Sunday, right after we re-signed our contract with the realtor.

This particular Sunday, a woman came forward and read a verse from Isaiah 54—a chapter that speaks of enlarging the place of your tent.

She said, "It's time to roll up the tent and see your dreams. Don't be afraid of them. Don't be afraid to expand and move or try what you haven't before. Your tent is being replaced with a bigger and better one, and it connects with the dreams in your heart, so don't be afraid to walk it out. Today is the day to pull up the stakes; there's an expansion of territory. The tent is related to the dream. Pack up the tent and receive the new one I have for you. It'll be easy."

Laura felt like she'd heard God say that He was in the sale of our house. We took this as another confirmation that God was in our decision to sell the house. We just needed to keep moving by faith.

With this, we made the decision to keep going and see what God would do through us in the sale of the house. Over the next couple months, more people came to look at the house. So many of them were amazed that we would sell such a beautiful house on the incredible land it sat on. It didn't take long for one of these couples to make an offer. On March 8, we finalized the contingencies of the sale and signed the contract.

All that was left was to line everything up to begin the process of getting ready for the move. We'd already picked out an apartment that we would move into for the first year. Actually, we'd signed up for two apartments back in October the previous year, which worked out to be a major blessing because Elise moved back in with us from college because of COVID-19. Now she would have a place to stay with us. I contacted the apartment complex and signed the agreements to start the leases in the middle of April. We could gradually move in our stuff before the final day of the sale in May.

Around this same time, Laura and I decided that we wouldn't start building the new house right away. We wanted to make sure that this was the right thing to do since we were in the middle of COVID and the market was so volatile. We questioned if this was what God wanted us to do anyway.

I am so thankful for the things that God spoke to us these couple different times because, during the process of packing and preparing to leave the house, I found myself questioning, *Are we doing the right thing?* Then I'd remember the times that God spoke to us and could keep moving in the direction of selling the house.

On May 3, we took the last little bit of stuff we needed to move and left our house of sixteen years for the last time. It was a very hard day for us, and there was a lot of crying. However, we knew that this was what God allowed us to do and that we could only move into our next season of life if we were willing to let go of this one.

At 9:00 a.m. on Monday, we signed the papers to sell the house. We were now officially living in the apartment and on to the next great adventure to see where God would take us.

I wish I could say that this was an easy process and an exciting time for us. But it was one of the hardest things I've ever put myself or my family through. But because we were certain that we'd heard from God on this, I knew we'd made the right decision.

The Bible tells us that God speaks to us with a still, small voice. Isaiah 30:21 says, "Whether you turn to the right or left, your ears will hear a voice behind you saying, 'This is the way, walk in it.'"

I've learned this very lesson. God does speak to us in this still, small voice, and it's up to us to sharpen our ears to hear what He's saying and believe that He has spoken to us. Just like with the sale of our house, the things God says to us may not come all at once but at many different times in many different ways.

When we question if we actually heard from God, this either comes from our lack of faith or is a question that comes directly from Satan himself. Satan doesn't have any new tricks up his sleeve. He's been making us question God since the beginning of time.

The Bible tells us that God created a man and a woman, Adam and Eve. When He created them and placed them in the Garden, God gave them everything necessary and beneficial for them to have a wonderful, fun life.

God told them they were to "Be fruitful and increase in number; fill the earth and subdue it. Rule over the fish of the sea and the birds of the air and over every living creature that moves on the ground."

Then God said, "I give you every seed-bearing plant that is on the face of the earth and every tree that has fruit with seed in it. They will be yours for food. And to all the beasts of the earth and all the birds of the air and all the creatures that move on the ground—everything that has breath of life in it—I give every green plant for food" (Genesis 1:28–30). And it was so.

The Lord God took the man and put him in the Garden of Eden to work it and take care of it. And the Lord God commanded the man, "You are free to eat from any tree in the garden, but you must not eat from the tree of the knowledge of good and evil, for when you eat of it, you will surely die" (Genesis 2:15–17).

God gave Adam and Eve an amazing place to live. He put them in charge of everything He made, and they had the right to do as they wished and eat whatever they wanted. They lacked nothing that would totally satisfy them and make life a pleasurable experience. There was no reason for them to question if God spoke to them, but they did question Him because they were deceived. Genesis 3:1–5 says:

Now the serpent was more crafty than any of the wild animals the Lord God had made. He said to the woman, "DID GOD REALLY SAY you must not eat from any tree in the garden?" The woman said to the serpent, "We may eat fruit from the trees in the garden, but God did say, 'You must not eat fruit from the

tree that is in the middle of the garden, and you must not touch
it, or you will die.' "You surely will not die," the serpent told the
woman. "For God knows that when you eat of it your eyes will
be opened, and you will be like God, knowing good and evil."

God always allows us to have choices in life. We can trust in
Him and live, or we can reject Him that He has the best for us
and die. Adam and Eve had a choice to believe that what God
had told them was the truth and for their good. However, in
the same garden that God created, the serpent would deceive
them. The Bible tells us that God is love. True love is not controlling, but it allows for the choice to believe or not believe
that what God has said is the truth.

I believe that God allowed the serpent in the Garden of
Eden because He loved these two people so much that He
wanted His words to be enough for them to believe Him. He
did not place the serpent there but allowed the serpent to be
there for their benefit, so they would trust that what God had
told them was for their good.

In much the same way, many of us hear God say something
to us in either an audible way or in the subconscious mind. We
then usually begin to act on this, and almost every time, we
hear a voice in our head that says, "DID GOD REALLY SAY?"
Satan has no new tricks; he still comes to deceive us and tries
to steal, kill, and destroy what God has spoken into being. We
must get to the point that when we hear God speak to us in
whatever form, we trust what He says and that is enough for us.

For Laura and me, our moment of trust came when we
heard my friend John say that sometimes we need to step out

in faith and then watch what God will do. If we hadn't taken a step of faith and acted on the prompt to put our house up for sale, we'd still be questioning if God wanted us to sell the house. It wasn't easy for us to sell the house; this was the dream house we'd built for our family. But who are we to question something that God tells us to do? "Faith comes by hearing and hearing by the word of God" (Romans 10:17 [NKJV]). We need to speak His word into our life, so we can audibly hear His word to have faith in what we heard Him say to us.

It's not unusual to question if you've heard from God, and there are some things you can do to help yourself when you're questioning. The first thing I do is to go back and ask God if this prompt was from Him. When I pray, I say this: "God, if You are in this decision, please open the door wide for me to see it open or close the door shut." When I've prayed this prayer, and I let go of control, He's been faithful every time to guide me through the decision I need to make.

It's not unusual to question if you've heard from God, and there are some things you can do to help yourself when you're questioning.

If the door doesn't shut, it's time to step through it. God loves us, and if we truly trust in Him and refrain from moving on something that's simply our desire, He will determine our steps. The Bible says, "In his heart a man plans his course, but the Lord determines his steps" (Proverbs 16:9).

I've also learned that faith is a verb, not a noun. Verbs mean action. By not moving, you aren't trusting that God will be in the step you are taking. But when you do move according to what you feel you heard God say, you learn to trust Him to speak into your life. Your sensitivity to His voice will grow stronger, and you'll begin to trust even more in His voice.

Don't second-guess what you hear Him say. Trust that God has the best for you and that what you feel is the Holy Spirit prompting you to move. You'll be able to stand firm in your decision because you'll remember the time and place that you heard God speak to you. He's always faithful to fulfilling what He set in place.

Finally, the Bible tells us to put on the full armor of God. One of these pieces of armor is the Helmet of Salvation. Helmets are made to protect our heads from the attacks of the enemy. When we put on the Helmet of Salvation, we protect ourselves from the voice of the enemy that speaks lies to us. This helmet protects by the Word of God that is truth in our lives.

With practice and listening closely, you can be more assured that you've heard from God. Listen to that inner voice and trust that God only has good for His children. When you hear Him tell you to let go, move in faith that He has the best for you.

3

I DON'T WANT TO LOSE CONTROL

A favorite TV series that Laura and I like to watch in our downtime is *American Pickers*. In this show, two guys travel around the United States looking for hidden treasures that others have collected and held on to for years. These two men, Mike Wolfe and Frank Fritz, created an entire series out of looking for people who've collected massive amounts of stuff. And how do they find these collectors? Either someone tells them about the collectors, or they pull up to homes that have a lot of stuff strewn around their property, much of which looks like junk to me.

I've watched this show for years, and it amazes me that these collectors (better known as hoarders) aren't willing to let go of the stuff that's sitting in their yard collecting rust. Maybe they once dreamt of what the items could be if they restored them, but life happened, and they never got around to it. But—and this is what strikes me as odd—they're unwilling to let go of these items, so someone else can restore or beautify them. It really has nothing to do with the amount of money they'd receive if they let the item go. It's that they can't see their item in someone else's possession.

I think the reason they can't let go is out of fear, fear that they'll no longer be in control of what happens to that item. Many of us may do the same thing. We're afraid to let go because we're afraid we'll lose control. It is actually downright scary for some of us to think about what it would be like if we weren't in control of a situation, a relationship, or even our future.

> *I think the reason they can't let go is out of fear, fear that they'll no longer be in control of what happens to that item.*

When Laura and I were married in 1993, we agreed to wait five years until we started a family. I wanted children right away, but Laura thought we needed time to bond as a married couple first. Though it was hard for me to let go of the idea of having children immediately, I recognized the wisdom in waiting.

Fast forward to 1998. Laura and I were at church one Sunday morning. Toward the end of the service, our pastor approached us and asked if he could pray for us. He said that there was something he felt God wanted to speak to us. I don't remember everything he said, but I do remember that he asked if we were pregnant. I looked at Laura, and Laura looked at me. We replied that if we were pregnant, we didn't know anything about it. The pastor said that God's message to us was that the baby was going to be OK and would be healthy when he or she was born. I thought that was odd.

A month later, we decided to add some new trees and landscaping to the new ranch house we'd built the previous year. It was a very hot week, and it was incredibly exhausting to work out in the hot sun. That Friday evening was our fifth wedding anniversary, and we decided to work on the yard during the day, then celebrate that evening by going out for dinner and to a local fair. We ended our yard work early and started getting ready for the evening around 4:00 p.m.

Before we left, Laura said, "I need to go get my present for you. Sit on the couch, and I'll be right back."

I wasn't happy about that because we'd agreed not to get each other a gift. I was a little bothered that she'd gotten me a gift, and I'd only thought to get her flowers. Then she walked out of the spare bedroom with a little baby doll down by her tummy.

"I wanted to give you this for our fifth anniversary," she said.

Clueless and still annoyed about her getting me something, I said, "A baby doll?"

"No," Laura said. "We're having a baby."

That took a while to sink in. When we got to the restaurant, I finally realized that we were going to have a child. Wow!

As the months passed, I got more and more excited about the child who would be a part of our family. I wanted to know if we were having a boy or a girl, but Laura wanted to wait to find out until he or she was born. In order to honor Laura's wishes, I had to let go of needing to know the sex. We'd both be surprised on the day of the birth.

The nine months flew by, and Laura woke up one morning with birthing pains. We headed to the hospital around 5:00

a.m. We lived about thirty minutes from the hospital, and as any man would think to do when his wife was getting ready to deliver the baby, I drove the speed limit the entire way. At the hospital, they ushered us to a delivery room and began monitoring Laura and the baby.

"I want to have this baby naturally," Laura said. "Please don't give me the epidural."

Everything was progressing as it should. Laura was doing well, and every time we took a walk up and down the hall, she seemed to progress even further. But around 2:00 p.m., her progress halted.

The doctor said, "It really is OK to get the epidural. There's no need to feel bad about giving birth that way."

Laura wasn't ready to give up. But around 3:30 p.m., the doctor said he'd be leaving for the evening.

He asked her one more time, "Would you like to consider getting an epidural? If this goes too far, we won't be able to administer one at that point."

Laura let go of the desire to have a natural childbirth, and an hour later, the anesthesiologist administered the epidural. I cannot confirm or deny if I passed out when he did this, but I do remember getting up out of the chair after the shot was given and not being able to recall everything that just happened!

At 7:10 p.m., our daughter, Elise, was born. She needed to eat right away, and Laura always wanted to nurse our children. At first, this went as well as it could for both of them. Laura worked hard to learn everything she could from the lactation nurse to make it a success. Yet, it seemed that Elise wasn't getting all the food she needed. Nevertheless, they sent us home that Friday evening.

For the next few days, Laura worked with Elise to breast-feed. She tried every trick they told us. But as new parents, it was frustrating for all three of us. The next week, we went back to see the lactation nurse, concerned that Elise wasn't getting enough milk. This nurse pushed Laura to keep trying.

But then another nurse came in. She told Laura, "If at some point you feel the breastfeeding isn't working, and you want to supplement with formula, it's totally fine. You shouldn't feel guilty about doing that."

Laura didn't want to give up this healthy way to feed her baby, but in the end, she wanted what was best for Elise. She tried to nurse for many more weeks but ultimately decided to move to formula. It wasn't easy to let go of her dream of nursing her baby, but it was the right decision, and Laura handled it well.

As Elise grew, I felt more and more responsibility to protect and care for her. I had a deep concern about keeping her safe, and I wanted to protect her. I continually cautioned her to be careful about things I thought could hurt her or draw her in the wrong direction.

I taught both the girls to ride bikes, climb trees, and even ride horses, but eventually, I felt responsible for bigger things, like making sure they knew the right way to go in life and how to make decisions—such as when to date and where to go to college. My girls were still little, so I watched how other older parents set parameters for their children. I observed

45

what worked for them and wondered if we should mimic their approach.

Now that I'm older, I have the benefit of hindsight, and I know that what you see on the outside may not be what's actually going on. There are many things that parents do to protect their kids, but sometimes parents overprotect their kids and try to maneuver every aspect of their lives in order to reach the dreams *they* have for their kids. The hazard in this is that many children live out their parents' dreams rather than their own. Some parents say they're raising their child in the way they should go, but the decisions they make for that child are made out of fear or a need to control how he or she functions in life. We set rules that seem to be for the child's benefit, but the rule is actually a way to control the child because we're afraid they won't make wise decisions on their own.

I grew up around church leaders who were very direct, and they expressed what marriage should look like and how children should be raised. They never actually sat parents down and directed them to raise their children a certain way, but as someone who was taught that leaders were chosen for their position by God, who was I to dispute the things that I learned? On the other hand, I adopted some of these ideas as my own, believing that this was the best course for my children.

For example, when Elise was still young, I began hearing different ideas regarding children and dating. I listened to a lot of opinions about dating from people I really respected and thought I should examine what those parameters would look like for our girls.

It was clear that parents had different views about when was the right time for kids to start dating. One of the ideas I embraced was that the purpose of dating was for marriage, which I still agree with somewhat today. Kids normally start dating without knowing their actual purpose in dating. Dating is simply a way to get to know another person to see if they'd be the type of person—or even the actual person—they'd want to marry one day.

I asked a close friend of mine for his opinion. He said, "A good measuring stick for the time to begin dating is when that person is ready financially, emotionally, and spiritually."

I thought that was very sound, well-grounded. As I thought about when that might be, it seemed like the late college years would be a time when a person would be ready financially, emotionally, and spiritually. What I didn't consider is that, though this might be good for one person, it may not be the proper measuring stick for all kids.

I knew I had plenty of lead time for teaching our girls when they could start dating. I didn't have to set a certain age, but I could give them this parameter that they could embrace as well. I wanted to set this in their minds at an early age so they'd know the rules of dating when the time came.

I think Elise was around eleven or twelve when we started talking about dating. One evening, I brought up the topic of dating after dinner. I wanted to explain to Elise and Raquel, who was only six, my thoughts about dating. So, I opened the conversation.

"Girls, when do you think is a good time to start dating?"

Elise said, "I'm not sure. Maybe sixteen?"

"That may be a time as far as age goes," I said, "but the purpose of dating is to get to know if the person you're dating is the type of person you'd want to marry. So, if you're dating for marriage, would you get married at sixteen?"

"I guess not," Elise answered

"So, what would be a good time to start dating if it is for marriage?"

"I guess like twenty?" she said.

"Since dating is for marriage, a good time to start dating is when you're ready financially, emotionally, and spiritually. So, when would that be?"

"I'm not sure," Elise said.

"A good time to begin thinking about dating would be when you're ready financially, emotionally, and spiritually; that would probably be after high school or even toward the end of college."

And that became the rule in our house. Laura went along with it because that's where we were in life at the time. I'm the one who brought this measuring stick into our household, rather than actually working this out together and listening to what Laura thought about it. I thought I was protecting the girls from getting hurt and helping them stay on course for where they should go in life.

Elise entered high school, and I felt sure that our parameter would keep her safe and prevent her from getting hurt by guys who could break her heart. I thought dating in high school was wrong because kids didn't have the emotional ability to handle such a big decision. The more they dated and broke up, the more it would set a pattern that when things got hard in a relationship, or if you didn't like what someone was doing, you could break up with them and move on to another—a dangerous pattern they would carry with them into marriage. In reality, what I was trying to do was control my children because I was afraid of seeing them get hurt.

Then there was the matter of college. I thought about all the kids I knew who'd struggled with their families or walked away from church life in their college years. I'd heard stories of kids who went off the deep end, and I felt that the best way to help my girls was to keep them close to home, so I could still have time with them and monitor any changes in their attitudes or behavior. If they started to change, I could step in and get them back on the right path.

> *In reality, what I was trying to do was control my children because I was afraid of seeing them get hurt.*

In her sophomore year of high school, Elise began looking at colleges where she might like to apply. I told her she could go to any college in the United States as long as it was within thirty miles of our house. Yes, this was kind of a joke, but I really wanted her to stay close to home. Elise, on the other hand, wanted to go to college in California or Florida.

As the process progressed, we started to have friction in our relationship. I tried to control her—and the decisions she should have had the freedom to make on her own. The Bible says, "Train up a child in the way he should go, and when he gets old, he will not turn from it" (Proverbs 22:6).

Instead of trusting Elise to make the right decision on her own, I wanted to drive her college decision. I was trying to control her out of fear.

In February of Elise's junior year, I sat near the front row of the church. It had been a good morning within the family, and I wasn't thinking about Elise's future or the decisions she was making. But as we started singing a worship song, a question began to form in my mind that I believed God was asking me.

"When did you dedicate Elise to Me?"

In our church, we celebrate the birth of a child by dedicating him or her back to God. The child dedication was a symbolic ceremony where we promised to raise the child in the ways of the Christian church. Its roots are found in the Bible, when Hannah promised God that if He gave her a boy, she would dedicate him to serving God.

When I heard God ask, "When did you dedicate Elise to Me?" I replied verbally, "We dedicated her when she was a couple weeks old."

"What did you do?" He asked

I said, "We took her up on stage."

"What happened then?"

"The pastor prayed over her," I answered, "and other couples prayed for her."

"What happened after that?"

"We walked off the stage and sat in our seats," I said.

Again, He asked, "What happened after that?"

"Um, we raised her in the best way we knew how."

Then God said, "When she was born isn't when you truly dedicate her to Me. You need to dedicate her to Me today when she is grown. When she was a little baby, you verbally dedicated her, but you still had to feed her, change her diapers, protect her, and raise her. But to truly dedicate her, you must let go of your control over her today, when she's grown and doesn't need you to survive. Now is when you dedicate her to Me."

I began to cry because letting go isn't easy for a parent. I said, "Fine. If I do this, You have to promise to take care of her."

"I took care of you, didn't I?" He replied.

At this, I had nothing more to say except, "I promise that as of today, she is Yours. I relinquish any control over her life."

I didn't tell anyone about this conversation with God. I kept it to myself and wondered what it all meant. About a month later, I was cleaning the stalls in our barn. I pushed the manure wheelbarrow down to the pile behind the barn and dumped the load. As I was pushing the wheelbarrow back to the barn, I heard God speak to me again.

"What if she wants to date?"

I actually yelled back, "That's not fair!"

He said, "When did you dedicate her to Me?"

I said in a very firm and loud voice, "FINE, but You have to promise to take care of her!"

Again, He said to me, "I took care of you, didn't I?"

I'm sure some people might question if God really spoke to me. All I can say is that I wouldn't have made this up, nor would I have been able to let go of controlling Elise on my own. But I had learned that God is wiser than I could ever be. The Bible says in Isaiah 30:21, "Whether you turn to the right or to the left, you will hear a voice behind you, saying, 'This is the way; walk in it.'" This is exactly what happened to me; this is how I heard God speak to me.

Earlier that year, I'd told Elise that if she was asked to a dance, we would consider letting her go, but she needed to ask us first. Up to this point, discussions about boys had never come up. But a few weeks after I heard God question me about dating, that changed. I was sitting in my bed around 10:00 p.m. watching TV when Elise came into our bedroom and sat next to me.

She looked over to me and said, "Can I ask you a question?"

I don't know why I responded this way, but I said, "Yes, you can go to prom, and no, he cannot drive you."

With shock in her voice, Elise said, "How'd you know I was going to ask you that?"

"God told me," I said.

"Really?" she asked.

"Yes."

"Did He really?" she asked, a little amazed.

"No," I laughed. "It was just a good guess."

Then I said, "Actually, we need to wait and talk with Mommy (this is what Elise still called Laura) first."

Laura came in a few minutes later, and Elise asked the question again. We agreed that, of course, she could go to prom.

"However," I told Elise, "I want to meet the guy you're going with. And he's not allowed to drive you." I had known of a few people that had crashed the night of prom and died. I wasn't ready to let another sixteen-year-old drive my daughter to prom.

Elise accepted these requirements with amazing maturity. She arranged a time for me to meet this young man, JJ Simon, at a local restaurant before school one morning. As I got to know him over breakfast, I really liked him. I gave JJ my permission to take Elise to their junior prom.

A few weeks later, I headed off to Haiti on a mission trip. While I was in Haiti, Elise talked to Laura about how much she wanted JJ to be able to drive her to the prom. Elise began praying that I would give my permission.

A few weeks before the big night, Elise began to lay out the plan for prom day. She would go to the salon to get her hair done, then get her nails done, pick up the boutonniere, and then come home and get dressed. Laura and I would take pictures of Elise at our house, then take her to the park, where she'd meet up with JJ and the rest of her friends for pictures. After pictures, we'd drive Elise to the prom, which was about five miles from the park.

A few days before prom, Elise asked, "Would it be OK if JJ drove me to prom—and if not from the house to the park, could he at least drive me from the park to prom itself?"

This time, I thought I'd let go of trying to totally control this and said, "Yes, I think that would be fine." This wasn't easy for me, but I needed to learn to trust Elise with the decisions she was making for her life.

Elise went with JJ to prom and had an amazing time. He wore a white suit, and Elise wore a beautiful blue gown. They truly looked like a prince and a princess heading to a ball. Over the next couple months, JJ spent more and more time at our house. He was really good at math, and he helped Elise with her honors math class.

> *This time, I thought I'd let go of trying to totally control this and said, "Yes, I think that would be fine."*

Toward the end of May, they began to look more like a dating couple than just friends. One Saturday, late at night, I told Elise, "Your relationship with JJ is starting to look more like a dating relationship than just friendship. If you guys are going to date, I'd like him to speak to me first about this, so we're on the same page about what that relationship will look like."

Elise agreed and said she wanted to text JJ right then, so she was clear about exactly what I expected.

"Would you mind letting me know what you want him to do?" At her request, I began dictating what she should type. She was really nervous, and halfway through, she said, "Would you just type in what you think I should say?" So that's what I did.

The following day, I saw that JJ had texted me around 7:00 a.m.

His text said: *Mr. Kassebaum, could we get together to discuss Elise and my friendship?*

I replied: *Yes, but I am headed out of town on Tuesday, so I am not sure how soon you would like to get together.*

JJ replied: *How about today after church?*

I texted back: *That would be fine.*

Then JJ asked: *Would it be OK if my father joined us?*

I texted back: *Of course, that would be totally fine.*

That afternoon we met at the local Red Robin restaurant—just JJ, his dad, and me. We ate and talked about life and sports for a while.

After about an hour, I said to JJ, "Is there a reason we're here, or is there anything you want to ask me?"

JJ replied, "Yeah, sure. Would you give me permission to date Elise?"

After a thirty-minute discussion about what dating meant to him, what he thought the purpose of dating was, and laying out the parameters of their dating relationship, both Dave and I gave our permission for JJ to ask Elise to begin dating.

About a week later, they went out for the first time, and JJ asked Elise if she wanted to date him. Elise absolutely agreed with a big YES!

In the fall of 2016, Elise started her senior year of high school. Over the next six months, she also began the process of selecting a college. Elise had thought she wanted to go to college in another state; however, all the colleges she looked at were in our home state of Missouri. One that I hoped she would consider was Lindenwood University. It was first on my list but last on Elise's.

She toured six different campuses, and in February, she made a decision. After looking at everything each school had to offer in terms of helping her get the degree she wanted, as well as the living conditions of each one, she had narrowed it down to her favorite. Without any influence from Laura or me, Elise chose Lindenwood University.

I'm so proud of how Elise walked through these difficult years with a father who wanted to control every aspect of her life. Though, at the time, I felt I was so involved because I wanted the best for my daughter, but I was really trying to control her because of my fears.

I'm so proud of how Elise walked through these difficult years with a father who wanted to control every aspect of her life.

In fact, if I hadn't listened to God, Elise may not be the strong godly woman she is today. I was interfering with her growth process, and I could have lost my close relationship with her altogether. Though this was one of the hardest and most challenging times of growth for me, I'm so thankful that it came sooner rather than later in life. Today, Elise and I have a much healthier and stronger relationship because I've learned to back off from controlling every aspect of my life and other people's lives. The only way Elise could become all that God has for her was for me to step away from the control panel of her life. I've learned to only share my thoughts when requested, then support others with the decisions they make.

Control issues are nothing new. We see this very same scenario played out in the Bible between Abraham and his nephew Lot. Genesis 13 tells us that Abraham had left the Egyptians and become very wealthy. Lot traveled alongside Abraham for a long time and acquired wealth and herds of animals as large as Abraham's. When all their families, their livestock, and their herdsmen began to move throughout the land, quarreling began between Abraham's herdsmen and Lot's herdsmen over the available grass and water.

Because of this, Abraham felt it best that they part ways. He told Lot that for the sake of peace between everyone, they should go in separate directions. In Genesis 13:9, Abraham told Lot, "If you go to the left, I will go to the right; if you go to the right, I'll go to the left." He allowed Lot to decide in which area of land they would live. Abraham could have insisted on keeping control of the entire situation and skewed everything in his favor. He had every right to do so because he was the head of the family. But Abraham humbled himself, released control, and gave the decision to Lot.

Lot saw that the Jordan area had the best grass and water for his flocks. The cities seemed like they would be a great place for his family to live. So, Lot chose the Jordan region, which was to the east, and Abraham went west to the land of Canaan.

God then spoke to Abraham and told him that he should look to the north, south, east, and west. As far as he could see was all the land that God would give to him and his offspring, forever. God greatly blessed Abraham and all his descendants.

I believe that Abraham was blessed by God because he was willing to listen to God, to move where God wanted him to move, and do what God wanted him to do. Abraham didn't try to control every situation or person he came across. He held loosely to the things before him, and God richly blessed him.

There are some practical steps you can take to start letting go of the need to control. In doing so, you'll find a deeper peace as you relinquish the results to others.

The first step is to release control in one area that you feel won't cause you much pain. For me, it was when I decided to step out of the college decision. I let Elise do the research and decide which one was best for her. By that, I gained freedom from the decision process, and at the same time, Elise was empowered to make her own decision. When you let go of this first thing, it enables you to let go of the bigger things. You'll gain confidence in God and His ability to work out all things for your good.

If you don't relinquish control of something in your life, you're committing a sin before God. In essence, you're saying to God, "I've got this. I don't need Your help." This is pride, and pride is a sin. When you release to God that one thing you desire most, you release the pride of controlling the outcome. Similar to me thinking that Elise needed to choose a college near home so I could monitor her attitude, I was telling God, "I'll watch over her. You don't need to."

When you release to God that one thing you desire most, you release the pride of controlling the outcome.

God is who gives us the desires of our hearts, like my desire for my daughter to be well during her college years. It was up to me to release this desire back into His control. I was never in control anyway.

The second step is to sit down and speak with the person you think you need to control. Release them! I had to do this with Elise and JJ when they wanted to date. When I spoke with JJ over lunch, I asked, "What are the parameters of dating?" I mentioned what I thought some of the parameters should be, but both Elise and JJ needed to talk about what those would be for them because they were accountable to God for each other. In the end, I had to release their relationship to both of them to work out because I wasn't accountable to God for their relationship, they were.

When you discuss the parameters of your relationships, you're both empowered to communicate on a deeper level rather than having a dominant/subservient relationship. And that's what happened with Elise and JJ. They defined the parameters for each of them, and now they both understand what the other expects and needs from the other.

Go ahead; I dare you to let go! When you let go of the idea of control, you can enjoy what you've been trying to control. It's a relief. I promise that you won't lose control but will gain deeper confidence to trust God in all things.

4

IF I LET GO, I CAN'T GO BACK

When I grew up, my family lived on eight acres in a rural part of the Saint Louis area called High Ridge. We had our house, a barn, a pond, and a couple horses. There were no neighbors near us, and it felt very secluded. Only one other person my age lived near us. His name was Ralph, but we called him Frog because he wore green boots and loved to jump in puddles.

Our family didn't have a lot of money, but what we had was precious: freedom to do what we wanted. Because it was so secluded, my five siblings and I all hung out together. We loved to play kickball, soccer, tag, and football. During the summer, we did the chores early in the morning, then had the rest of the day to do whatever we wanted. We could go anywhere and pretty much do anything we wanted. Many summer days, we got out the horses and rode for hours, exploring the woods and nearby areas. We investigated the caves and caught catfish in the river. Sometimes we helped the local farmer load his hay wagons with the hay that was cut for the winter.

During winter, we made long toboggan runs in the deeper snows, winding them down the tractor paths through the woods. At night, we took five-gallon buckets of water and dumped them down these paths, and the next day they'd glisten with ice and were extremely fast. We used pieces of rolled-up hard plastic and rode the paths over and over. And it was fast! Someone always ended up getting hurt in some way, and then we'd have to go inside for the rest of the day. We had so much fun doing these things, just the six of us.

My dad was the local barber, and everyone knew him. He was also involved in the community, and he coached the boys' baseball teams that my brothers and I played on. As a family, we'd take long walks and talk about God and life. My parents made doing things as a family a high priority, and I appreciated that as I grew up.

My mom's parents lived a few miles up the road from us, so we got to see them any time we wanted. My grandfather loved pigs, and my grandma loved her grandkids. She was always doing fun stuff with us or teaching us card games. I really enjoyed hanging out with them.

When I was around six years old, my parents decided to turn their lives over to God. It's what we call *being saved* in the Christian church. It meant that they stopped pursuing their interests in life and started pursuing the desires God gave them. With this change, they started attending a new type of church about forty minutes away, rather than the local Catholic church that was close to our house that we'd attended since I was born. They became very involved in this nonde-nominational church, and I think we attended almost every event possible. Many of the people I met at that young age are still in my life today.

As we got a little older, there were more and more events going on at the church. With about 1,000 members, there was always something to attend. As my brothers and sisters got older, they started driving, so we could get out more and do things farther away from home. Though we loved the property where we lived, it was becoming a chore to live there instead of being a fun place to live and enjoy family life. The house and barn were getting older and needed repairs, but as my parents got more involved in the church and a new business opportunity, there was less time to fix them.

When I was eleven, we had a family meeting, and my parents talked about selling the house and moving closer to the church. I was torn. I really wanted to move to be closer to my friends, but I didn't want to move because I was finally getting old enough to do just about anything around the property without anyone's help or permission. I could drive the tractor and take the horses out on my own. It was every eleven-year-old boy's dream.

About a year later, my parents got a contract on the house. Everything was now set in motion to move out of this season of our lives and into another season where we lived in the city. And we would be just two streets away from one of my best friends.

As moving day drew closer, I began worrying that we were letting go of this place that had made us the family we were. We'd never be able to come back and do the things we'd done for so long because another family was moving in. They were even buying the tractor and the horses that I loved to ride. I could never go back and have them for myself.

I took it pretty hard on the day of the move. My parents and friends spent the day loading trucks and trailers and moving everything to our new house. I was heartbroken and didn't want to leave. Mom and Dad let us ride the horses up until the very moment that we had to leave. I'll never forget my last time walking our horses, Rosey and Rusty, into the barn and saying goodbye to them. I held on to their necks for such a long time. I knew that when I let go, I would never have them as my own again. But, of course, I couldn't stay there all my life and hold on to them. I eventually had to let go, and when I did, it was with anguish.

As we arrived at our new house, the pain of leaving the old house slowly started to fade. When I made the conscious decision that this was my new home, I got more and more excited about the new area and exploring everything around me. I didn't know it at the time, but I learned a great lesson that day that would help me when I got older and had to make a similar decision: When you let go of something, there really is no going back. Thirty-six years later, I went through this same test of letting go of something I could never return to. And it would be one of the hardest things I have ever experienced.

I didn't know it at the time, but I learned a great lesson that day that would help me when I got older and had to make a similar decision: When you let go of something, there really is no going back.

In June of 2019, Laura and I had decided to sell

our property where we'd raised our two daughters for the previous fifteen years. We'd built the house, the barn, put in the pool, and had made this a dream property. We enjoyed everything about it, except all the work it took to keep it looking so nice. We had spent five years upgrading and adding to the house to make it exactly what we wanted, but we felt God telling us it was time to move into a new season of life. We needed to trust Him in this, and that meant selling the house.

Elise had already moved out and was living on campus at the university. Raquel was getting older and would finish high school and move on to the next stage of her life. We knew God was doing something in us, and it was time to let go of this dream and move on to another.

We listed the house in the summer of 2019 and got a contract on the house in March of 2020—exactly when COVID-19 hit and everything started to lock down. We were told to "shelter in place," to stay home unless it was absolutely necessary to go out. However, we were in the middle of a sale and had much to do to prepare for the move—like hiring a moving company. Ordinarily, this was easy to arrange, but because of all the new parameters to keep their workers safe during a pandemic, the timeline to schedule a move was pushed out further and further. I finally found a company that had what we needed. They could move us on the day we needed, and they had the necessary team members to do it.

Next, we wanted to sell the things that we would not be taking with us to our much smaller apartment. Because of COVID-19, you couldn't have garage sales, so I became the king of selling stuff online. I constantly made trips to deliver things that people purchased or met them at gas stations for the delivery. Many of these were easy to let go of because we didn't need them, but others, like the girls' childhood toys, were harder.

We also started boxing everything up and sorting which things we'd move into the apartment and which to move into storage until we could decide what to do with them. We marked the boxes with an A for the apartment and a B for storage.

Everything was harder to do and much more time-consuming because of the pandemic. Because we were so busy and focused on the move, I never had time to think about what we were leaving behind. Not that I wasn't aware that we were moving our family out of the house and off of the property, but I didn't ever have time to stop and look around at all we were leaving behind.

The move wasn't the only big event happening. Our oldest daughter Elise was turning twenty-one on April 28. Her special birthday was five days before we walked out of our house for the last time. Elise had thought about what she wanted to do on this special birthday for a long time, but because of the pandemic, she couldn't do any of those things because all the venues were closed, and her college friends had moved back home to other states. We needed to make this birthday as special as we could while, at the same time, preparing to move out.

Laura and I wanted our home to be as normal as possible for Elise's big day, so we couldn't take anything apart or move anything out of the house quite yet. Laura had always been so great at making the girls' birthdays special, and she didn't miss a beat on this one either. She thought of some special things we could do for Elise even though many places were closed.

On April 28, I left the house early to pick up the cake we'd ordered from the local baker. (Thank you, Jesus, that they were still open. I guess that's why the bakery is called Heaven Scent Bakery!) While I was gone, Laura hung decorations in the kitchen. Elise eventually woke up and spent the next hour getting ready for her big day. She dressed in a special outfit for the day and came down the stairs with me snapping pictures the entire way. JJ, her boyfriend, was there, and after we celebrated as a family, he took her to enjoy some special things he'd arranged for a fun day of celebration. Later that afternoon, he dropped her off at a local hotel to meet up with her best friend, Amanda, to have a fun night of celebrating together.

It was a momentous time for us to get together and enjoy the fun that we'd had in this home for so many years. It was a special day for the entire family. COVID-19 had interrupted so many celebrations—and even what Elise had originally planned. But Elise let go of that plan and had a wonderful, fun-filled twenty-first birthday.

On April 29, we took down all the birthday decorations and began preparing for the movers to come the next day. We had a lot to do and a short time to do it: take all beds apart, take down the TVs, get all of Elise's and Raquel's stuff out of their rooms, move the freezer out of the basement, bring everything up from the barn, make deliveries of stuff we'd sold or were giving away, and so much more. We were very busy preparing to make the next day as smooth as possible.

At 8:30 a.m. on April 30, two moving trucks arrived. While the movers were doing their job, we tried to stay out of the way. We wanted it to go as fast as possible because we were paying by the hour. After a couple hours, our neighbors across the road came over to give us a going away gift. They were and still are the best neighbors that we could have prayed for. They had welcomed us into their community from the first day we met, and they taught me so much over the years. To leave this community, knowing we wouldn't be going back, hit me hard that morning. The movers finally had everything loaded, and we headed first to the storage unit to drop off a load and then on to the apartment to deliver everything else.

The next day, Friday, professional cleaners came and cleaned the entire house. At the same time, we were still removing items that we'd wanted to move ourselves. I was still selling things on Facebook and making those deliveries. Our apartment was unorganized, so we began putting a few items away. We ran back and forth from the house to the apartment all day long.

By the time Saturday rolled around, most of the stuff had been moved out and was in the apartment or in storage. We still had a couple of trailers full of stuff to take to the apartment on Saturday or Sunday, the day we would finally leave. But Raquel had asked if she could have some friends over to enjoy the pool for the last time, similar to me riding our horses for the last time when my parents sold their house.

We'd had some issues with the pool for the couple weeks leading up to this day, and I'd worked hard to make sure the pool was in working order for both the new owners and for

Elise and Raquel to enjoy their last full day at the pool. After the girls had finished their time in the pool and their friends left, I walked around the house looking for stuff we'd missed. I noticed two stones that we'd made with the girls when they were younger. They'd put their hands in the cement and then decorated around their handprints with jewels. We'd put these in a back garden area next to the walk to the pool. That's when a rush of emotion finally came over me. Now the realization of all the memories hit me hard.

That night, I thought it would be fun to build the girls a bonfire in the fire pit one last time. As we sat around the fire, we relived the memories of the previous sixteen years. We talked about all the funny and special moments of living in such a wonderful place. Raquel told us how much she loved the fire pit and how, on her previous birthday, she and two of her friends had sat around it until late into the night discussing life and God.

Finally, I left the fire for the last time. I went inside and sat on the couch that the new owners had bought from us. I was flooded with overwhelming emotions that built up, realizing the kindness of God for allowing us to live this dream life. At the same time, He was urging us to let it go to pursue something new He had for us, but we didn't know what it was. It reminded me of a story in the Bible of Jesus and the rich man.

> *As Jesus started on his way, a man ran up to him and fell on his knees before him. "Good teacher," he asked, "what must I do to inherit eternal life?"*

"Why do you call me good?" Jesus answered. "No one is good—except God alone. You know the commandments: 'You shall not murder, you shall not commit adultery, you shall not steal, you shall not give false testimony, you shall not defraud, honor your father and mother.'"

"Teacher," he declared, "all these I have kept since I was a boy."

Jesus looked at him and loved him. "One thing you lack," he said. "Go, sell everything you have and give to the poor, and you will have treasure in heaven. Then come, follow me."

At this the man's face fell. He went away sad, because he had great wealth. Mark 10:17–22

I thought about this incident that happened 2,000 years ago and felt God's kindness upon me. He whispered about how proud He was of Laura and me to let go of something that had been our dream and go where He was calling us. Our response was the opposite of the rich man in the story; we were willing to let go of this house to pursue Him.

I felt a lot of raw emotions, and I wanted others to know what we were walking through. The night before we left our house for the final time, I posted this on Facebook:

May 2, 2020

Today is a pretty special day in our family. Today we spend the last night in this house where we grew as a family. Almost exactly sixteen years to the day, we broke ground to build this house.

So many memories were made in this home that will never be forgotten. But God has been so very kind to us. He has developed us into the family he wanted us to become in this house.

But now we move on to the next chapter of our life in an apartment. You see, the thing I have learned the most in this house is the kindness of God on our lives when we let go of the things we thought we wanted the most and grab onto the things that God wants most for us.

I loved living in a big house, but I love more running after a big God. He has NEVER let me down, NEVER failed me, NEVER left me, NEVER walked away from me, but He has asked me to do one thing: let go of all that I desire and go after Him.

Now we are doing that again, letting go of this house to let the next family enjoy the pleasure of what God has allowed us to have.

So today is really hard for me because of all that God has done for us here, but I thank God for all that He will do through Laura, me, and our two daughters in the years to come.

It was really good for me to think through and write down my thoughts because it defined the kindness of God toward me. At the same time, it reminded me that He was in control of the next season of our life. Even though the next season was undefined, it allowed me to restate my trust in God to determine our steps for our future.

Even though the next season was undefined, it allowed me to restate my trust in God to determine our steps for our future.

I woke up early Sunday morning after sleeping on

71

the floor where our bed used to be. I made a cup of coffee and sat on the back porch that overlooked the pool, barn, and the rest of our property. I'd done this so many times before. It was here that I read the Bible and prayed. Many times, I'd wake up the girls early, and we made breakfast, then sat and read a book together. This would be my last morning to sit on this porch and enjoy what God had given us.

About an hour later, Elise walked out and sat in the chair next to me. We didn't really have a very strong relationship then because, as I said before, I was trying to hold on to my little girl, and she was emerging as the woman she was meant to be. As we made morning small talk, Elise said something that I know could only be God.

"What you and Mommy are doing reminds me of the story of the rich young ruler in the Bible. He asked Jesus a question about eternal life, but he couldn't let go of his possessions to actually follow God. But you two are following God and are willing to let go."

That's exactly what God had shown me the night before. Only God could have orchestrated Elise walking out and mentioning the same thing He'd spoken to me the night before. There's a certain thrill in knowing you're following God, and yet, I still felt a deep sense of loss because I knew we would never be able to go back. But you can't get to your destiny if you remain stuck in the past.

From Raquel, I learned that though you let go of one area of your life and may never go back, there's always something better in the future—if you let go. Raquel was experiencing everything we were in selling this house, but she had hope for herself in the new place we were moving to. She was excited about her new room and the opportunity to design it in any way she wanted. She looked forward to watching the Superbowl on a big screen at the apartment complex. She was also happy about being closer to all her friends. Raquel taught me the art of flexibility when you aren't in charge of the change. She taught me that if you learn to let go well, you don't have to mourn what you left behind.

. . . you can't get to your destiny if you remain stuck in the past.

We'd decided to be ready to leave our home for the final time by 4:00 p.m. that Sunday, but by 1:00 p.m., we had everything packed up and were ready to leave. The house was so empty.

We took pictures, and I told the girls they could write their names or anything they wanted to say on hidden places in the house that only they would know. It was fun to do this but also incredibly sad. It was beginning to hit me that we'd never be able to go back to this house or this time again.

About an hour before we left, I sat on the couch, reflecting on some memories. A few minutes later, Laura came in and sat next to me, then Elise and Raquel joined us. I suggested that we pray and thank God for this time. I didn't expect the emotions to overtake me. As soon as I began to pray, I broke down and cried. As I wept, I prayed the following out loud:

"God, You have been so kind to us. And for that, we say Thank You!"

"God, You gave us this house to live in. And for that, we say Thank You!"

"God, You allowed us to be a family here. And for that, we say Thank You!"

"God, You taught us who You are while living here. And for that, we say Thank You!"

"God, You allowed us to have horses and learn to ride. And for that, we say Thank You!"

"God, You gave us amazing sunrises and sunsets. And for that, we say Thank You!" I kept praying these types of thankful prayers to God.

When I finished, Elise said, "You know, Daddy, when Raquel and I walked into this house, we weren't Christians because we were little at the time. But we've given our hearts to Jesus, and when we walk out, we'll walk out as Christians." Wow, this was so good for me to hear, knowing that God not only had us in our decision but all our hearts as well.

We went out on the front porch to get one last photo, then went to our cars. Elise was driving her car, Laura and Raquel were in Laura's car, and I was driving my truck. We all cried as we pulled away. I pulled past the front of the house and stopped. I rolled down the window and choked out, "Goodbye."

I knew then that I'd let go of something that I couldn't go back to. I cried almost the entire twenty-minute drive to our apartment. When I got to the apartment, I thought, *We just let go of one season, and we will now pursue another. There's no going back, so we need to look forward to what God has for each of us.*

On Monday morning, I woke up early. In just a couple of hours, we'd sign the papers that would finalize this chapter in our life. Laura came out and said she was ready to go.

She knew that this final act was weighing on me and asked, "Are you sure we should do this?"

So many things ran through my head about wanting to back out of the sale. But I said, "We have to. If we back out, it wouldn't be fair to the family who's buying the house, the real estate agent who put so much effort into selling it, and worse, Elise and Raquel, who've been through so much with the move."

At this, I broke down and walked into the bathroom to collect myself. I was struggling so much, and it didn't make sense to me because I knew this was the right decision. But I just couldn't get over the finality of the decision. I texted both my parents and our pastor and said, *Please pray for me. I am really struggling.*

With that, Laura and I headed to the closing. When we arrived, I was doing much better, and I was able to compose myself during the entire signing.

After we left the building and got in the car, Laura asked, "How are you doing?"

With that, I broke down one last time. The papers had been signed, and we would begin the next season of our lives. It felt so odd that we'd decided to let go of something, and it was painful to do so, yet at the same time, I knew that if I didn't do this, I couldn't move into the next phase where I needed to go.

We stopped to get Starbucks for Raquel on the way back to the apartment. It was getting close to lunchtime. The apartment was packed with stuff, and we had no place to sit except on the bed that I'd put together for Laura and me.

Raquel and I loved to watch Andy Griffith together, so we turned on the only TV we had, which was on our dresser in our bedroom. Raquel began watching a show while I made a small bowl of noodles and vegetables.

It felt so odd that we'd decided to let go of something, and it was painful to do so, yet at the same time, I knew that if I didn't do this, I couldn't move into the next phase where I needed to go.

I headed into the bedroom to sit on the bed and watch a quick show with her, but I needed to move some things out of the way first. I was holding the bowl of noodles in my left hand. As I grabbed something with my right hand to throw it off the bed, I turned and hit the bowl of vegetables in my left hand. It flew out of my hand; the food jumped out of the bowl and down on the carpet at my feet.

Something in me broke. I fell to my knees and began to cry hard. All the emotion that had built up inside poured out. I walked back into the kitchen to get supplies to clean up the mess.

"Do you want me to clean up the food?" Laura asked.

"No, I have to do this."

I had to do it to get through something I was dealing with. I walked over to the spilled bowl, knelt down, and began picking up one pea at a time. I felt so depressed, and I said to God, *You have to help me do this.*

That evening, my friend, Mark Bartig, stopped by to pick up a small desk that he'd bought from me. He and his family had just sold the house where they'd raised their children and moved into another house. He was so excited about the new house and their new neighbors. It was the complete opposite of my experience, although I'd felt that same excitement until a few days earlier.

We went outside, and I told Mark everything I'd gone through that day.

"I feel like I'm going through a deep depression over this decision, and it's really weird. I know this is what we should do, but it's such a painful thing to go through."

Mark's answer was wise. "Derrik, I believe you're going through a great grieving time. Unless you let that thing that you've held on to die, you can never go into the next thing that God has for you. It's similar to grieving a death. You must let the grief run its course to go forward."

Mark asked if he could pray with me, and he asked God to help me grieve and find peace to move forward. With that, he put the desk in his truck and left.

The feeling of loss left me. I'd almost reached the door of the apartment when I stopped and said

Unless you let that thing that you've held on to die, you can never go into the next thing that God has for you.

out loud, "If we are going to do this, we must be intentional about the things God has us do here."

When I walked in, Laura asked, "How are you doing?"

I looked at her, and with something near joy in my voice, I said, "I'm really good. Mark just talked to me and helped me understand what I was going through. My grief is gone, and I feel fine."

From that point forward, I've never felt grief about not being able to go back to our old home, our old life. I was ready and excited for the future.

The Bible tells of two people who made the decision to let go of something. The first story is about a man named Elisha. When Elisha lived, kings and leaders went to prophets for advice when they had to make hard decisions. Prophets were known for having an intimate relationship with God, and they were both feared and revered.

One of these prophets was Elijah. Elijah had been prophet to the Israelites for a very long time. He was zealous for God, and at the same time, he'd been dealing with the Israelites and their rejection of God's covenant. In fact, except for Elijah, they'd killed all the other prophets. He'd been running away from them when God stopped him and spoke to him about what he was doing.

God told Elijah to go back and anoint three men. He was to anoint Hazel as king over Aram, Jehu as king over Israel, and Elisha to proceed him as prophet. So Elijah set out to do just as God had told him to do. We pick the story up in 1 Kings 19:19–21.

> *So Elijah went from there and found Elisha son of Shaphat. He was plowing with twelve yoke of oxen, and he himself was driving the twelfth pair. Elijah went up and threw his cloak around him. Elisha then left his oxen and ran after Elijah. "Let me kiss my father and mother good-bye," he said, "and then I will come with you."*

"Go back," Elijah replied. "What have I done to you?"
So Elisha left him and went back. He took his yoke of oxen
and slaughtered them. He burned the plowing equipment to
cook the meat and gave it to the people, and they ate. Then he
set out to follow Elijah and became his attendant.

When Elisha was anointed by Elijah to be the next prophet, there wasn't a loud or grand announcement. Elijah simply put his cloak around Elisha, and Elisha knew that he was to leave everything behind and follow Elijah. Though the Bible doesn't state this, I think Elisha was probably praying to God and asking what He wanted from him, which was when Elijah came and put his cloak on Elisha.

It's interesting to see Elisha's response. He IMMEDIATELY stopped what he was doing, ran to Elijah, and said, *"Let me kiss my father and mother good-bye," he said, "and then I will come with you."* He then went back and killed his oxen and burnt his plow. When God called Elisha into the office of a prophet, Elisha cut off every opportunity to go back to his old way of life.

The second example is a story about Lot and his wife. Lot and his wife lived in a city called Sodom. This is where they chose to live after Abraham and Lot parted ways. Lot chose the best land for himself and his herds, and Abraham went the other direction.

Sodom had become a very wicked city. It had become so bad that God sent two men (angels, we believe) to spy on the city to see if there were any righteous people who lived there. When they arrived at the city gate, they met Lot. Lot immediately invited these two men into his home for dinner. He knew that these men must be from God.

After they ate, they were all getting ready to lie down to sleep when many men from the city came for the two visitors. These men were so wicked that they told Lot to send his two guests out so they could have sex with them. Lot was afraid for his guests, so he went outside and offered his own daughters for the men to have sex with.

The men got hostile toward Lot. The two guests sent from God pulled Lot back inside the house and warned him that they were going to destroy the city. Lot would be allowed to flee with his relatives, but no one else could join them. The two men grabbed Lot, his wife, and his daughters and removed them from the city.

> As soon as they had brought them out, one of them said, "Flee for your lives! **Don't look back**, and don't stop anywhere in the plain! Flee to the mountains or you will be swept away!" But Lot said to them, "No, my lords, please! Your servant has found favor in your eyes, and you have shown great kindness to me in sparing my life. But I can't flee to the mountains; this disaster will overtake me, and I'll die. Look, here is a town near enough to run to, and it is small. Let me flee to it—it is very small, isn't it? Then my life will be spared." He said to him, "Very well, I will grant this request too; I will not overthrow the town you speak of. But flee there quickly, because I cannot do anything until you reach it." (That is why the town was called Zoar.)
>
> By the time Lot reached Zoar, the sun had risen over the land. Then the LORD rained down burning sulfur on Sodom and Gomorrah—from the LORD out of the heavens. Thus he

overthrew those cities and the entire plain, destroying all those living in the cities—and also the vegetation in the land. But Lot's wife looked back, and she became a pillar of salt. Genesis 19:17–26

Lot and his wife had found favor from the two visitors for their kindness. The two men were spying on the city for God but ended up helping Lot escape because Lot had protected them. But then Lot and his wife did two things to hold on to the past rather than letting go and moving into what God had for them.

First, Lot tried to negotiate to stay in the land that he had once chosen for himself. The two men were trying to save Lot, but he couldn't let go and trust that God had the best for him. It's only my opinion, but I think he wanted to go to the next city, Zoar, so he could go back to this region one day.

Second, Lot's wife looked back. Most of us might think, *What's wrong with looking back?* Here's the thing: Lot's wife was *specifically* told not to look back. She disobeyed what God's men told her to do. She had to see the place she once lived one more time. She didn't trust that letting go would be best for her. For her disobedience and lack of trust, she was killed and turned into a pillar of salt.

Both Elisha and Lot's family had been given the opportunity to move in a new direction in their life. Both opportunities required that they trust that what was being offered was for their good. Elisha cut off every opportunity to reverse the decision he'd made to let go and trust God. Lot and his family, though they eventually went in the direction God asked, tried to hold on to the past, and that cost them a family member and the better life that God had planned.

One of the first things I learned to help me let go without looking back is to do something similar to Elisha. Determine where to draw that line in the sand and then step over that line. For me, the line was after I spoke with Mark; I chose to be intentional in whatever God had for us in this new season in our lives. I drew a line in the sand and decided not to look back in regret (it is OK to remember the joy we had as a family in the house) about what we had to leave behind. By making a firm decision that you're going to move past the line, you'll find that the way forward is more peaceful and freeing than the place you were in.

Next, start telling others about your decision. Telling others will put your decision in motion. Once the process forward begins, one thing will lead to another, and you'll move out of any discomfort. The excitement builds, and others will cheer you on to keep going in the right direction. Once we made the decision to sell the house, we started telling others what we were doing and why we were doing it. This allowed us to keep moving forward without the ability to go back.

DON'T LOOK BACK! If you look back, you'll second-guess your decision. Look forward so you can see new opportunities and focus on the destiny you were meant to live. If you look back in any way—with longing or revisionist memories about how good things used to be—it's a sign that you haven't let go. To this day, I absolutely loved the time of raising our family in that house. I couldn't have dreamed of a better way for us to do it. But I also never look back in regret because

I know we made our decision in faith that God was leading us into a new season of our lives.

Letting go of something that has meant so much to you is never easy. However, the only way forward is to be intentional in the decision you make without looking back in regret.

5

DOING THIS DOESN'T MAKE SENSE

In the early 1990s, Sonja Dickherber started going to Haiti on an annual mission trip with a dentist named Dr. Paz to provide dental care for the Haitian people. They traveled to La Gonave, about forty miles from the inner coast of Haiti. Sonja fell in love with the people and looked forward to her annual trip.

In fact, when her husband Jerry decided that he was ready to retire, he asked, "What should we do now that we have all this time on our hands?"

Sonja quickly replied, "I'd like to live in Haiti for a year and serve the Haitian people."

Jerry, an avid hunter and fisherman, agreed. "If that's what you want to do, I think we should do it—as long as the fishing is good."

A change like this wouldn't make sense to a typical couple moving into their retirement years, but that's what Sonja and Jerry chose to do.

When they arrived, they began serving in a local ministry where Sonja had previously worked with Dr. Paz. After a few months, Sonja started feeling restless. The mission didn't allow them to leave the compound during the day. The only contact they had with the locals was when they came to the mission grounds to receive healthcare or education.

Sonja and Jerry decided to move out and find a place of their own. They rented a small, dark, one-room apartment that had no windows near the middle of town. It was very close to where Sonja had previously worked and right across the street from the busy local market. Though their apartment was hot and dark, it was perfect for what they were about to do.

Every night, Sonja and Jerry grabbed a fifteen-gallon metal pot and walked to an area called the Saline, about a half mile from where they lived. They made a fire under the pot and put together a meal of beans and rice for the local children, who often hadn't had anything to eat during the day. They served the meals night after night and began to form relationships with the people. They discovered there was a great need for a school and a medical clinic for the children. They weren't only starving for food; they were starving for medical care and education too.

Sonja and Jerry decided to fill that need. Through an amazing miracle that only God could have done, they were able to purchase five acres of land about two miles away. They could now begin the work that they believed God was directing them to do.

Every morning, Jerry, at age sixty-six, got up early and grabbed two eighty-pound bags of concrete, hoisting one on each shoulder. He walked two miles to their property and dropped them off, then walked back to get two more bags to take to the worksite. The next time, he went back to get shovels and buckets, and when he arrived at the property, he dropped the tools and walked a half mile up the hill to get water. Carrying the water back, he mixed the concrete to make mortar to construct their first building—a storage building. When Jerry completed the storage area, he started building a small, three-bedroom home where Sonja and he would live.

Sonja spent her days teaching six young men the Bible and leadership skills. The men had asked her to teach them all she knew about the Bible, leadership, and how to influence their community. She spent twelve hours each day in that small apartment—with little light and no airflow—teaching them all she knew.

During this same time, they'd invited a pastor from their church back in Warrenton, Missouri, to come visit. Sonja presented him with the opportunity to build a church, a medical clinic, and a school on the property. After much discussion, they decided to join forces to accomplish this vision. The church began sending volunteer work teams to help Sonja and Jerry build the church. When the church was completed, Sonja began holding services, and the church began to grow slowly.

In 2010, a massive 7.0 earthquake hit the mainland of Haiti. Jerry had just opened the door to walk outside when the earthquake hit. The force was so strong that it knocked him off his feet and down the front steps of his house. A few minutes later, the locals began arriving at the property. With no electricity or system of communication, the people were frightened and didn't understand what was happening.

Sonja and Jerry cared for them and let them stay on the property until it was okay to go back to their homes. As the days, weeks, and months passed, more and more resources were sent to help the people of Haiti, including money and supplies. With this infusion of cash and supplies, Sonja and Jerry began building the medical clinic to offer free care to children ages seven and younger.

At the advice of others, Sonja and Jerry moved back to the United States after the earthquake, but they traveled back to Haiti six or seven times a year to serve the people. Whenever they returned from such a trip, Sonja spoke at her home church to share about their most recent trip. My sister-in-law, Beth, was part of that congregation, and she felt moved to go to Haiti with them to help in any way she could. Shortly after her first trip, my brother, Don, decided he'd go with her the next time.

They told me stories of how Sonja and Jerry fed over six hundred children a day and offered free schooling to over three hundred. I started sensing that God wanted me to get involved in some way. Laura and I gave monthly donations to Sonja and Jerry's ministry, Celebrate Jesus of Haiti. Though I hadn't yet met Sonja and Jerry, I knew God was leading me to help.

In February 2013, I heard about a small group of five who were going to Haiti to help Sonja and Jerry enclose their twenty acres with a six-foot wire fence. They called this property the Promised Land because Sonja and Jerry had bought it to divide among thirty-two families in the church. Now they'd be able to grow crops on their partial lots and generate a sustainable income. However, because the cows and goats of the island roamed freely, they ate the crops the people had grown. The only way to prevent this was to put up a fence.

I sensed that God was leading me to go with this group. So, I contacted my brother to let him know I was willing to go, and he passed on my information to someone else in the group. Until the day we left, I'd never met any of the people who were going. In fact, I'd only briefly met Sonja and Jerry at my niece's wedding. I wasn't even sure where Haiti was. To say that I was nervous was an understatement. The questions started going through my head:

> What was I doing?
> Why did I say I would go?
> Would I fit in with this group?
> What would my role be?
> Would I get sick down there?
> Would I come home? (I seriously worried about that.)

There was no easy way to get to the island in Haiti where we were going. But soon after we met that early morning of the flight, I began to sense I was going to be in charge of helping the group in the travel down to Haiti. We left Saint Louis and flew to Miami, arriving late at night, so we had to spend the night at an airport hotel. Again, I felt that I was able to help lead the group because travel was what I did, and the others seemed OK with me leading them. We were up at 4:30 a.m. the next morning to catch our 7:30 flight to Port-Au-Prince,

Haiti. When we arrived in Port-Au-Prince, we gathered all our bags. (We'd brought a total of fifteen bags with items for the people of Haiti.) A lady named Donna, who'd been to Haiti one other time with Sonja, did her best to get us through the customs inspection. But since I'd done this so many times in my travels to other countries, I was able to step in and help lead the group through this. I was finally finding my role as the leader of the group—at least, that's what I thought. We left the airport in two vans and drove a mile to the other end of the airport, where we boarded a very small propeller plane that flew us to the small island of La Gonave.

When we landed on the dirt airstrip, I saw two white people in the middle of a large group of black people who were waiting at the other end of the airstrip. As we deplaned, the rest of our group was greeted by Sonja and Jerry as though they were old friends. I, on the other hand, didn't even recognize them. However, they both welcomed me warmly.

Most of our bags fit into the back of the old, black Toyota pickup. We put the rest on people's motorcycles who had come to help with our arrival. As for us weary travelers, we piled into the back of the pickup, the luggage jammed between us. The roads were incredibly rough, so our speed topped out at fifteen miles per hour.

On the way to the mission, whenever we passed a group of children who were walking or standing by the side of the road, they got big smiles on their faces and chased after our truck, singing out, "Pastor Sonja, Pastor Sonja, Pastor Sonja."

It was so beautiful, but I thought to myself, *Why are they singing the name Pastor Sonja?* This seemed so odd, yet it was also so beautiful. It happened over and over whenever we passed the children.

We arrived at the main property around 1:00 p.m. after twenty-four hours of travel. We quickly unpacked and ate lunch, then set out for the property, so we could determine what our fencing project would involve. Again, children ran alongside the truck and sang, "Pastor Sonja, Pastor Sonja, Pastor Sonja!" Again, I wondered, *Why are they calling her Pastor Sonja?*

When we arrived, we saw that the Haitians had already built the corner poles for the fencing. Now we had to figure out the best way to stand them up and lay out the six-foot-tall wire fencing. Everyone seemed to have an idea. Since I'd been a leader in our travel to Haiti, I thought I ought to step up as the leader of the project too, and I began to talk to them about what we needed to do to get the fence up.

Very quickly, however, I learned who would be the leader of this project, and it wasn't me. A man named Dave, Donna's husband, moved around quietly and began putting things in the order we needed to build the fence. He had a skill that I didn't have. He began working and moving stuff around as if he knew how it was supposed to be. I quickly moved aside and watched Jerry and Dave figure out what needed to be done.

As I stood under a small tree and waited for them to decide the best way forward, I felt God say to me, *It's time to give up the leadership you had of this group. There are others who are better skilled at this project. It's time for you to just serve them.*

Wow, I was only the leader of this group for a short twenty-four hours. However, if we were going to get the project done in the few days we had, I'd have to let go of my pride and let those who were gifted in the work lead the project. God will use who He needs to fulfill His desires.

We worked all afternoon and finally headed back to the guest house around 5:30 p.m. Again, as we headed back, the children ran alongside the truck and sang, "Pastor Sonja, Pastor Sonja, Pastor Sonja!" Not the sharpest pencil in the pack, I still wondered why they were calling her Pastor Sonja.

On Saturday, we woke up early and headed out again for the Promised Land. This time, Sonja stayed back to have meetings with some of the people who ran the church and the mission. We didn't have any children running alongside us, but many of the people we saw along the way yelled Jerry's name. "Jerrryyyy! Jerrryyy!" But they never yelled "Pastor Jerry" like they did with Sonja. This really troubled me.

We got a lot accomplished that day because the right people were leading. After eleven hours, we called it quits for the day, and I was exhausted. The others laughed at me because I curled up on a small couch and slept while they talked into the evening. As far as I was concerned, I was either working or sleeping. I was happy to hear that we wouldn't be working on Sunday.

On Sunday, we all walked down the hill from the house where we were staying to the church that was already half filled with about two hundred people. The worship team led everyone in singing while people kept coming for the next forty-five minutes. When the time came for the preaching, Sonja stood up and went to the front, and with Pastor Juaquim interpreting for her, she gave a powerful, encouraging message. Afterward,

I was confused and kept thinking to myself, *Why was Sonja the one preaching? Why wasn't Jerry preaching?* I had assumed that Jerry was the preacher since he was a man.

I grew up in a church where men were always the leaders. The women performed the support roles. To see Sonja as the leader and preacher in the church didn't make sense to me. I know this wouldn't have bothered many of you, but coming from my background, Jerry would have been leading the building project *and* preaching and leading as the head of this church. This was why I was confused to see Sonja up front.

> *To see Sonja as the leader and preacher in the church didn't make sense to me.*

Later that evening, it hit me that the children addressed Sonja and Jerry as who they actually were. Sonja was "Pastor Sonja," and Jerry was just "Jerry"—her biggest support. I sat on the front step of the house with the bright stars all around me and asked God, *If it is right for a woman to be a pastor and head of this church, would You help me to let go of my old way of thinking and understand how Sonja could be both the pastor and leader?*

I heard God say, "I am God, and I am no respecter of person. I don't always do things the way that people teach they should be done. I choose the leaders who I choose to lead."

God was working on both my heart and my way of thinking. I was beginning to learn a big lesson. I needed to let go of my way of thinking and step into God's way of doing things. If I couldn't accept that Sonja's role was to be a pastor to these people, how could I accept what God was calling me to do? I decided that I wouldn't be bound by what others taught me was the truth but would, instead, let go of my old ways of thinking to pursue what God said in His Word.

We completed our project ahead of schedule and got to spend the last day with the people of the island. As we interacted with them, I had a lot of time to reflect on the many things that God did through me and in me that week. The biggest lesson I learned on the trip was to trust God when He speaks, even if it doesn't make sense.

> *I decided that I wouldn't be bound by what others taught me was the truth but would, instead, let go of my old ways of thinking to pursue what God said in His Word.*

A year later, Laura and I felt it was time to leave the church we'd attended for the first twenty-one years of our marriage, the church I'd been part of for thirty-eight years of my life. We knew God was leading us to pursue Him over the pursuit of a church.

In June of that year, we began attending a start-up church that had been around for nine months and was a lot closer to home. It was similar to the Sunday morning structure, but the spirit in the gathering was different. The first Sunday morning, I felt the presence of God on me in a way I hadn't felt in a very long time. It was so real and overwhelming that I began to cry during the worship time. I was embarrassed about this and turned to face the wall almost the entire time during worship.

Soon afterward, I started meeting with Tom Kyle, the pastor. I asked him about different things that I'd begun to question. Tom was always very gracious and kind in helping me walk through my questions. He never gave me an answer to any of them but would ask me questions that directed me to find the answers on my own.

One of my questions was about women in ministry. My confusion was still lingering from my time in Haiti the year before. Tom and I talked about many of the passages in the Bible that explained the roles of men (husbands) and women (wives). He pushed me to dig deep into these passages to discover what God's heart and His intentions for the church were in each of these passages.

As I began to dig into this question, I learned many things about who these passages were written to, the different cultures from which they were written, and the time when they were written. God began to reveal not His heart for women in ministry but His love for ALL His people. God's love for us and our love for Him is always the deepest desire He has for us.

I really struggled with this new way of thinking. But if I was going to progress, I knew I had to let go of my idea of being right because of what I had learned from others.

God began to reveal His desire for men and women collectively as *one people*, and He would give me understanding when I was studying or thinking about this subject. Two specific instances in 2014 stand out as being major turning points.

The first instance was when I was driving to pick up my girls from school one afternoon. I was listening to a podcast by a man who was teaching about women in ministry and how God was no respecter of person—even gender. This guy clearly had a different view from what I'd been taught through my years in the church. I started thinking about how

I'd always told my daughters that they could be anything they wanted to be. I tried to encourage them to go after whatever it was that they wanted to do in life. While I was thinking about that encouragement, a thought came to me about something that had happened the previous year. A teacher at a men's meeting had said, "A woman can be a leader in different ways, but the Bible is very clear that women are not to be the authority leader over men." This was at the time Nancy Pelosi became the US Speaker of the House. He continued with, "There is no way that a woman will ever rule over me in the church."

I felt God ask me this question: "What would you say if one of your daughters told you they wanted to run for president? How would you respond to them?" This question hit me hard because this new view of women in leadership didn't square with the way I was brought up. I asked myself, *How can this be a correct view of leadership when, for thousands of years, it was taught that men are the ultimate authority in the church?*

I began to hurt inside. How could I offer my girls the world but at the same time believe that there was a limit to how far God would use them? It caused me great pain that I would say one thing—that they were capable of anything—when I actually believed something else—that there was a limit for them in God's church.

The second instance was in the fall of 2014, when Elise started the ninth grade. I strongly encouraged her to get involved in a sport or activity at school. After trying a few different things, she took up golf. I thought she did this because she wanted to play golf, but later on she notified me that it was a two-month sport, and by playing golf, she wouldn't have to take physical education as one of her classes.

Elise was good at golf. All my buddies were amazed at how quickly she picked it up and how well she did. She excelled so much that she made it all the way to the district competition, which was held in the middle of Missouri, about two hours away from us. She left with the team on a Thursday afternoon before the meet on Friday. I drove out on Friday morning with plenty of time to watch her compete.

While driving, I listened to the first part of a podcast by a man who had done an in-depth study about God's intent for the roles of men and women. He began to break down the verses in the Bible that were commonly used to teach that men were to be the authority and women were not to speak in a leadership role in church. He showed the context of the time of the verse, the demographic of people it was written for (like Jew or Greek), how these people groups viewed women, and the issue that was being addressed in the full context of the verse.

As I listened, my understanding began to change. It made perfect sense to me. My desire began to change, and I wanted to see people in leadership roles as God directed them. How could my love as a father, who wanted everything in life for my daughters, ever be limited? God's desire for His children is never limited either.

Elise did very well that day. After the meet, she rode home with me, so she could get some homework done on the two-hour ride home. I listened to the second part of the teaching. About an hour into the drive, I felt this deep pain inside me. I needed to ask for Elise's forgiveness for teaching her that she was limited because she was born female. This teaching that women could not lead was degrading to women; it didn't lift women up to the heart of the Father.

With tears running down my face, I said, "Please forgive me for any time that I've taught you that you were less than a man because you were born female. I am so sorry if I taught you that you could only go so far with who God has designed you to be because you are female."

Of course, Elise said, "It's alright." We had a great discussion the rest of the drive home.

I learned a great lesson through the process of letting go of an internal way of thinking. We often think that letting go is a physical event in life, like with relationships or houses, but through this process, I learned that even when letting go doesn't make sense, we gain so much by allowing God to teach us about His true desires for us.

> *. . . even when letting go doesn't make sense, we gain so much by allowing God to teach us about His true desires for us.*

There's a Bible story about a man who was told to do something that didn't make sense to him. The Israelites had gone astray and were no longer living the way God had told them to live. Because of this, God removed His favor from the Israelites, and they were oppressed by the ruler of the Midianites. Every time the Israelites planted crops, the Midianites invaded their land and destroyed all the crops, forcing the Israelites to flee to the caves.

This happened year after year, and finally, the Israelites—through Gideon—cried out to God for help. But the manner in which Gideon was chosen didn't make sense to him.

Judges 6:11–16

The angel of the LORD came and sat down under the oak in Ophrah that belonged to Joash the Abiezrite, where his son Gideon was threshing wheat in a winepress to keep it from the Midianites. When the angel of the LORD appeared to Gideon, he said, "The LORD is with you, mighty warrior."

"Pardon me, my lord," Gideon replied, "but if the LORD is with us, why has all this happened to us? Where are all his wonders that our ancestors told us about when they said, 'Did not the LORD bring us up out of Egypt?' But now the LORD has abandoned us and given us into the hand of Midian."

The LORD turned to him and said, "Go in the strength you have and save Israel out of Midian's hand. Am I not sending you?"

"Pardon me, my LORD," Gideon replied, "but how can I save Israel? **My clan is the weakest in Manasseh, and I am the least in my family.*** "

The LORD answered, "I will be with you, and you will strike down all the Midianites, leaving none alive."

Gideon was chosen by the Angel of the Lord. He was not a head general, a leader in an army, a mighty warrior, or even from one of the larger, more popular clans. Gideon was clearly unqualified for the position. If they were playing a game of kickball, he would have been the last person chosen for the team.

Why was he unqualified? Gideon worked on the threshing floor of a winepress. He was only qualified to knock the heads of wheat off the stalk—a job that didn't take skill or courage. Additionally, Gideon's clan was the weakest in all the land. Furthermore, Gideon tells God that he is the least in his family.

It makes no sense that this person would be chosen to save all of Israel from the hands of the Midianites. Even though it didn't make sense to Gideon, it was God's will. God had chosen Gideon. Like Gideon, we often disqualify ourselves and try to make sense of why we are in a particular situation. Yet God works through the most unlikely to accomplish what He desires, whether they are male or female.

> *Like Gideon, we often disqualify ourselves and try to make sense of why we are in a particular situation. Yet God works through the most unlikely to accomplish what He desires, whether they are male or female.*

Gideon didn't believe what he heard from this angel. He began negotiating with the angel, asking for a sign that he had favor from God in this battle. He went back and forth, seeking assurance that he was who God would use to save the Israelites. With one last attempt, he asked God for one more sign:

Judges 6:36–40

Gideon said to God, "If you will save Israel by my hand as you have promised—look, I will place a wool fleece on the threshing floor. If there is dew only on the fleece and all the ground is dry, then I will know that you will save Israel by my hand, as you said." And that is what happened. Gideon rose early the next day; he squeezed the fleece and wrung out the dew—a bowlful of water. Then Gideon said to God, "Do not be angry with me. Let me make just one more request. Allow me one more test with the fleece, but this time make the fleece dry and let the ground be covered with dew." That night God did so. Only the fleece was dry; all the ground was covered with dew.

After this, Gideon felt assured that he had been chosen to lead the Israelites to victory. Gideon's courage and confidence were now high. He went out with all the Israelites to take on the Midianites. They set up camp and were ready to go to battle. Then God did something that would make even the most advanced military person stop and question the plan that was laid before him:

Judges 7:1–8

Early in the morning, Jerub-Baal (that is, Gideon) and all his men camped at the spring of Harod. The camp of Midian was north of them in the valley near the hill of Moreh. The LORD said to Gideon, "You have too many men. I cannot deliver Midian into their hands, or Israel would boast against me, 'My own strength has saved me.' Now announce to the army, 'Anyone who trembles with fear may turn back and leave Mount Gilead.'" So twenty-two thousand men left, while ten thousand remained. But the LORD said to Gideon, "There are still too many men. Take them down to the water, and I will thin them out for you there. If I say, 'This one shall go with you,' he shall go; but if I say, 'This one shall not go with you,' he shall not go." So

Gideon took the men down to the water. There the LORD told him, "Separate those who lap the water with their tongues as a dog laps from those who kneel down to drink." Three hundred of them drank from cupped hands, lapping like dogs. All the rest got down on their knees to drink. The LORD said to Gideon, "With the three hundred men that lapped I will save you and give the Midianites into your hands. Let all the others go home." So Gideon sent the rest of the Israelites home but kept the three hundred, who took over the provisions and trumpets of the others.

What a crazy story of how God would save Israel. God reduced His army from a full-strength military force to three hundred fighting men. Normally an army would go out with 50,000 to 100,000 military men.

We wonder how Gideon could have had the confidence to let go of his thoughts that this didn't make sense and proceed with the plan that God presented. But this is exactly how God works. He doesn't do things like we think they should be done. The Bible tells us that: "For my thoughts are not your thoughts, neither are your ways my ways (Is. 55:8)." After all, if we could do it on our own, God wouldn't get the glory. But if we let go of our ideas and do it God's way, when we have success, the only one who can get the glory is God.

When you come to those points in life where you need to let go of a certain way of thinking, like I did, or let go of the thoughts that the plan is too crazy like Gideon did, have the courage to move forward, even if things don't make sense.

There are some things you can do to help you through these times of letting go. First, ask yourself, *Who am I really trying to please?* When you're a Christ follower, your allegiance should be only to God the Father. If you're trying to please anyone else, then you haven't made God your only audience. You need to come to the point where you have an audience of one. Our goal in life should be to please God alone and give Him all the glory.

Paul asks a question to his readers in Galatians 1:10. "Am I now trying to win the approval of men, or of God? Or am I trying to please men? If I were still trying to please men, I would not be a servant of Christ." We may not be able to reach a logical conclusion in areas that don't make sense, but that's when we put our faith in God that He alone has the best for us.

Second, don't dwell on the past hurts caused by previous teachings. When you relinquish the wounds of the past, you can move into the future. I had to do this with the teaching I'd received regarding women in leadership. I now value the input women in leadership have had in my life more than I could have imagined. At the same time, the situation allowed me to communicate with my daughters with greater respect and love for them and the gifts God has given each of them.

Paul tells us in Philippians 3:13–14, "Brothers, I do not consider myself yet to have taken ahold of it. But one thing I do: Forgetting what is behind and straining toward what is ahead, I press on toward the goal to win the prize for which God has called me heavenward in Christ Jesus." Paul is clear that to take hold of our future in Christ Jesus, we must let go of the past, even past teaching that now doesn't make sense.

We must strive to find out what God's one true desire is. I can almost assure you that, at first, it will not make sense to you. Letting go is the only way we truly can reach the goal and the prize God has for us.

Finally, embrace these changes and new ways of thinking or living. History makers are those who challenge the status quo. Society moves forward by those who embrace the challenge of change. As you begin to move into the things that don't make sense, your faith in God to lead you strengthens. Your love for God will grow deeper and deeper. Jesus came into the world and challenged an entire people group—the Jews—in many areas of thought. Jesus taught that you do not please God by keeping the traditions, but to truly love God was to trust in Him by faith, even when things don't make sense.

> *As you begin to move into the things that don't make sense, your faith in God to lead you strengthens. Your love for God will grow deeper and deeper.*

The disciples followed Jesus for three years. During that time, He kept telling them how He was going to establish His kingdom. Yet when the time finally arrived, He warned them in the chapters of John 14–17 that He would be taken from them, that they would be on their own, and the world would hate them because of Him. That didn't make sense to the disciples. And they questioned Him about it. But this was the plan that God had for them and for us. God's desire is not that we understand or make sense of what He is teaching us but that we fully trust that His plan for us is good, even when it doesn't make sense.

Press through to trust that you are doing what God wants you to do when things don't make sense, and don't be afraid to make the changes you know you should make. Keep pushing yourself to let go of old ways of thinking, especially when it doesn't make sense.

6

NO ONE ELSE DOES THIS

One of my favorite quotes by Robert Frost says, "Two roads diverged in a wood, and I—I took the one less traveled by, and that has made all the difference." I love this quote because the people I admire the most make decisions that no one else would make. They've learned that if you're going to reach your full potential, you need to let go of the ordinary way of doing things and make the decision to be extraordinary.

I've come to those pivotal moments myself and have found that there are usually only two choices: the path that most people take and the path that seems irrational to others. I've learned to take the path that most people wouldn't choose.

I had twelve years of schooling, and not one of those years was enjoyable. They were all extremely painful for me as a student. I loved the extracurricular activities, but I absolutely hated going to school for learning. Every day was drudgery for me, and every night of doing homework was absolutely miserable. Few teachers challenged me to think outside the box of typical learning or understood that they could help each of us learn in the manner that best fit us as individual students.

Through no fault of their own, our teachers taught everyone in the same manner and expected us to learn the same way without realizing that there are many different ways of acquiring knowledge. This is an absurd way to help a young person learn to do what they are gifted to do in life. Many students like me who don't excel in a school classroom are labeled as average—or worse yet, failures—because we cannot excel in this type of system that was designed for teaching the masses as opposed to the individual.

As I entered my junior year of high school, my parents transferred me from a public school to a private school. I hadn't done well in the public school and started hanging out with a very rough crowd of kids. Though many teachers said I had a lot of potential, my grades and attitude in life didn't show it. Changing schools was a real struggle for me because of the actual change and because the new school was designed to prepare all its students for college. All I wanted to do was complete the last two years of school and never go back again. I had absolutely no interest in getting a college degree.

The message of that time was that in order to be a success in life, you had to go to college. We were told that you could get a job without a college degree, but you would never be a success in life without a college diploma. For someone like me, who hated almost everything about school, there was no way I'd sign up for four more years of this misery. And I was attending a high school that put benchmarks on how many of their students went on to college and what types of colleges they attended.

I must admit, I liked going to an all-boys school where I didn't have to worry about what girls were thinking about me or trying to impress them. I could relax and have a fun time with the other guys. There was a great sense of camaraderie and passion for the school. We also had a motto of "Men for Others," which would define my purpose later in life.

As I entered my senior year at seventeen years old, I had no clue what I wanted to do after I got out of school, but I was convinced that if I didn't go to college, I could never be a success. I believed that only losers and kids on drugs didn't go on to college, and since I didn't do drugs, I must be a loser.

All four of my older siblings had already gone to college and received their degrees or were in the process of doing so. I think my parents knew I wasn't interested in continuing that tradition.

Toward the end of my senior year, my father took me out to lunch to talk about what I wanted to do with my life. We went to a local restaurant, and he began to ask questions that very few seventeen-year-olds know how to answer.

"What do you want to do after high school?"

"What type of job do you eventually see yourself doing?"

"Are you interested in going to college?"

"If you don't go to college, what do you want to do?"

I really love my dad, and I appreciated the time he spent with me. However, I didn't have a clue about how to answer him. I just knew that I didn't want to go to college and that no one else I'd ever known had made that decision.

He wrote down the costs I'd incur if I went to college for four years and took out a loan to do so. I'd need about $36,000. When I graduated, I could probably get a job with a starting salary of around $25,000 to $30,000. So I'd be making around $27,000 a year—but I'd have a debt of $36,000.

I just knew that I didn't want to go to college and that no one else I'd ever known had made that decision.

On another piece of paper, he wrote out a different plan. I could graduate high school and get a job. If I stuck with that job and worked hard at it, after four years, I could probably make close to $20,000 to $25,000 a year. But after that four years, I wouldn't have any student loans. He also said that during this time, I could take a few courses about the job I chose, which would be like getting a specific education for the job I was really interested in.

By the time my father got to the second choice, I was sold. I now had my out from having to go to college. I knew this was the right path for me, but I still had a hard time letting go of the idea of college since no one else was choosing this course of life. All my friends and every other senior at my high school had chosen to continue their education.

On the day of my graduation, a priest from the school talked about the different colleges and career paths that the graduating students had chosen. He said, "We are so excited to announce that of the 187 graduating men this year, 186 of them have either applied to or been accepted into college."

I leaned over to the guy sitting to my left and said, "I know that one guy who did neither of those." By this time, I felt very satisfied that I was going to do life my way and not follow the crowd.

Though I was confident in my decision, I wasn't internally secure and struggled with the idea that the only ones who didn't go to college were either on drugs or were losers. A few weeks after my graduation, about twenty graduating seniors from our church had a get-together. I wanted to see everyone one last time before we all headed our different ways. As we gathered in our youth pastor's living room, he asked us all to tell the group what we'd be doing in the next stage of our lives. As each one began to share where they were going to college and what degree they'd be getting, I kept thinking, *No one else has opted out of college.*

I was so down on myself that by the time it was my turn, I said, "My name is Derrik. I'm not going to college because I'm a loser. I'm just going to work in my dad's company." I had no self-esteem at this time in my life.

As I began working for my dad, I was driving nearly 3,000 miles a week in a small minivan all over the East Coast, and I got tired of listening to music on the radio. Instead, I started buying tapes from motivational speakers. I began listening to people like Brian Tracy, Zig Zigler, and Lee Iacocca. Their teachings resonated with me and encouraged me that I could be something in life. There wasn't a single teacher in school, up to that time, who had ever told me that.

When I was out on the road, I parked in rest stops at night and would sleep in my van because we didn't have enough money for me to stay in hotels. I would just sit there and listen to these cassette tapes over and over. After working for my dad for a few months, I began to think about my life, and the old thoughts reentered my mind. *No one else does this.* But as I thought about that statement further, I took a different tone. *NO ONE ELSE DOES THIS!*

After a few months, I began to memorize Bible verses that spoke of me as a success in Christ. I started building excitement that I wouldn't live a life like everyone else, but I'd let go of the typical way of doing things and live an adventurous life because *NO ONE ELSE DOES THIS!*

From that time on, I had a new confidence in myself and faith that God had the best for me. I knew that no matter what, I was going to do life differently. I would take the road less traveled and try things that no one else would try.

> *I started building excitement that I wouldn't live a life like everyone else, but I'd let go of the typical way of doing things and live an adventurous life because NO ONE ELSE DOES THIS!*

Mathew 7:13–14 says, "Enter through the narrow gate. For wide is the gate and broad is the road that leads to destruction, and many enter through it. But small is the gate and narrow the road that leads to life, and only a few find it." As the years went on, I began to look for those hidden pathways and the narrow gates while trusting that God was letting me see these hidden pathways.

Over the next twenty years, there were many times that I looked for the path that no one else was taking. Sometimes, living this way got me into trouble, but more often, it allowed me to arrive at my goal while others were waiting for permission to move forward and wasting time. This way of life became natural to me.

One time I was working at a trade show in Orlando, Florida, with four other colleagues. It was a week-long event, and we arrived a couple of days early to set up, then worked the show on Thursday, Friday, and Saturday. It was an exhausting week because of the long hours at the show and then entertaining customers at night. By the time Sunday came around, we were all ready to go home.

Unlucky for us, a major rainstorm had hit the East Coast, and many flights were either canceled or greatly delayed. We arrived at the airport early on Sunday morning. Our flight was at 11:00 a.m., but we decided to get there three hours early because of the long lines we'd heard about. When the taxi driver pulled up to the area for departing flights, the line for the outside bag check was the entire length of the drop-off area. We thought we'd take our chances with the line inside the airport.

The line inside was longer, but we'd gotten there early and would wait our turn inside. I decided that one of us should go get the others coffee, and since it was my idea, I was selected. I got everyone's order and left the line to find a coffee shop.

Before looking for the coffee shop, I went back outside to see if that line was moving any faster. It was just as long as before, if not longer. I thought to myself, *I wonder how long it actually is?* So I climbed on top of a three-foot-tall concrete planter and looked as far as I could see. Something caught my eye that did not make sense.

Because I was living a life with the motto, "NO ONE ELSE DOES THIS!" I was looking for pathways and opportunities others may have missed. As I looked down the line, I noticed a gap, then another shorter line. I thought, *I wonder what that other line is for?* and walked all the way down to see why there was a shorter line. I saw that there were only about ten people in the line with three attendants helping them.

> *Because I was living a life with the motto, "NO ONE ELSE DOES THIS!" I was looking for pathways and opportunities others may have missed.*

I asked one of the attendants, "Can I check in for my flight here?"

"Yes," he said. "That would not be a problem."

"Why isn't anyone else coming down to this shorter line?" I asked.

What he said astonished me but made total sense when considering how the ordinary person thinks. He said, "Anyone can come to this line and check in, but everyone stops way back at the end of the other line because they don't take the time to look for another option. They're in a hurry, and if they would just drive down here, they'd see they could check in much faster down here. But very few people take the time to look."

With that, I stood in this short line and called one of my reps. "Bring the rest of the group and come outside, then walk to the very end of the drop-off lane. We can check in there."

He replied, "Why don't we just stay in line inside and wait our turn?"

"Don't say anything too loud, but tell everyone to come outside, and we can get checked in very quickly," I told him again.

"But if we leave, we'll lose our place in line," he replied.

This time I was much firmer and said, "Just tell everyone to follow you and come outside to the end of the drop-off lane. We're going to check in outside."

They arrived a couple minutes later, and we got checked in and had plenty of time to sit, relax, and have a nice breakfast in the airport before our flight. After we boarded our flight, some of the people who were ahead of us in line inside the airport came running onto the plane at the last minute. They were visibly distressed at having almost missed their flight.

I've told this story many times over the years to people when I try to explain that it's OK to try something different, even when no one else does it that way. As you begin to trust that God has the best for you, you'll find that it propels you faster to your next destination and many times without the stress. As Robert Frost suggested, look for the path less traveled.

The Company

I had just signed one of the largest retailers in the US, and we were getting ready to deliver them the largest order our company had ever shipped. Yet, over the next two years, I'd be challenged to do something no one else would do.

One of the first things coincided with a change in leadership within our company. My dad, my three brothers, and I had spent twenty-seven years building a brand of pet products.

We'd started in my dad's basement and had worked hard over the years to grow it into a multimillion-dollar business that sold products all over the world. It was a lot of work, and the brand Tropiclean was becoming a major player in the pet industry.

We were excited about the growth, but at the same time, each of us was getting more and more stressed in our own way. For me, it was beginning to feel like we were wandering around in the dark for many of the critical decisions we made. I think we were all afraid of letting go of what we'd built and the positions we held.

We appointed Landon Hobson, my brother Don's son-in-law, to be Director of Operations over manufacturing and the warehouse. Landon was new to the pet industry, manufacturing, the Midwest, our family, and the way we ran our company. Even without much experience in any of these areas, we thought he would play an integral role in our company in the years to come. In this role, he could begin to get his feet wet and learn the company from the inside out. Even though Landon didn't know the particulars of the pet industry, manufacturing, or the dynamics of our family, he brought his gift of servant leadership to the table.

Just a couple months after Landon started as the Director of Operations, my nephew, Bradley, invited me out to lunch. Bradley worked directly with me as an International Sales Representative, but over lunch, he told me that he'd been talking to his father (our CFO) and another of my brothers about stepping into the financial side of the business. I was really excited for him. However, I asked what education he had in finance.

Bradley said, "Only what I've learned from my father. I plan to go back to college and get an accounting degree."

I thought this was an interesting idea, and I was open to giving it a try.

As we made these changes in the company and allowed Landon and Bradley to take a more active role, others in the company asked me about the logic of what we were doing. After all, who puts novices in these key leadership positions? Landon and Bradley worked hard to earn the respect of the other employees and to understand their departments. They found ways to improve what had already been built.

Just six months later, their progress was accelerated even further because we had to make a change in the higher-level leadership of our company. We'd discovered that one of our top leaders had been dishonest. Because letting him go caused a gap in our leadership, we started to think about a plan for the future of the company, including its leadership.

We had to decide whether to keep going in the direction we'd been going, where my brothers and I led the company, or to seek out a new leadership model. If we kept going with us at the helm, we'd only have to replace this one individual. But that wouldn't give us the freedom to pursue new areas where God was leading each of us. If we wanted to change the leadership of the company, now would be the optimal time. Just one problem: We didn't know any executives who could fill these shoes.

There was a lot of discussion, and someone suggested that Landon become the CEO and Bradley the Director of Finance. This seemed logical because it would be a simple move, but neither of them had experience at this level. No one else would put two people who had little, if any, experience in high-level leadership positions and allow them to run a worldwide company. But that's exactly what we chose to do.

That November, we had a company-wide Thanksgiving lunch, where we announced that Landon Hobson would become the CEO and Bradley Kassebaum would be the new Director of Finance. Though they each lacked experience in their respective position, they were exactly the right people to take the company to the next level.

> *No one else would put two people who had little, if any, experience in high-level leadership positions and allow them to run a worldwide company. But that's exactly what we chose to do.*

Four years later, I can say that this was one of the best decisions we made. It wasn't the easiest decision to make, and it did come with some problems, but it worked. Landon and Bradley had to learn what our expectations were as the company owners, and they learned how to communicate those expectations to the rest of the company. And my brothers and I had to learn the tough lesson about how to let go of what we'd spent our whole lives building. It's a path that has made all the difference.

Our Home

I've already told you about letting go of our home, and I finally concluded that it doesn't matter what anyone else would do. I knew we needed to let go of that house and that season in our lives. Doing something that others wouldn't do helped us step into the next chapter that God had for us.

Over the next year of living in the apartment, we got to spend more time with each other than we had in a long time. We no longer had the stress of keeping up with the cleaning and maintenance of a large property. When I used to work around the house all the time, I always wondered what other people did while I was busy maintaining the property. Now I found out: They did anything they wanted to do!

A year after we moved, we realized another benefit of the apartment. We'd actually rented two two-bedroom apartments that were right next to each other. (By the way, no one else would do that either.) Our thought was that we could live in one of them with Raquel and have the other one as a place to entertain guests and small groups. It also gave us a place for a separate office. And yet, these apartments became a blessing in a different way for our entire family that we hadn't expected.

When Elise graduated college, she had the opportunity to go to Africa for an internship for a couple of months. On her return, she needed a place to stay. The second apartment took the stress off her needing to find a place to live right away, and at the same time, it allowed her to be on her own in a separate place from her parents. It allowed us to be close with our daughter and gave her the separation that a young adult needs. And at the same time, Elise and Raquel could be close to each other for Raquel's senior year of high school.

There are many times in life when we have to make hard decisions, and we may ask ourselves, *What am I doing? No one else would do this.* But we're not alone. There are countless stories in the Bible about people who did things in unorthodox ways.

Joshua

Joshua was selected by God to lead the Israelites into the promised land. Joshua and all the other Israelites had followed Moses out of Egypt and were headed to Canaan, the land that God had promised them. Many exciting things happened along the way that caused Joshua to trust in God's leadership.

Joshua saw Moses part the Red Sea, so the Israelites could cross on dry land, and then he saw this same sea close up on the Egyptians that chased them. Next, he witnessed God leading them with a cloud in the sky by day and a pillar of fire by night. And every morning, God provided them with birds and bread to eat. These miracles increased Joshua's faith in God to do what He said He would do.

As they approached Canaan, Moses sent twelve spies to research the land and its inhabitants. Joshua was one of the twelve that crossed over the Jordan River to spy on this unknown area. When they returned, they talked about all the amazing things that were in the land and how wonderful it was. They told of grapes that were as large as basketballs and said that it was a land that was teeming with milk and honey. However, ten of the spies (Joshua not included) also told stories of giant people who lived in the land. These ten convinced all the Israelites to fear the people who lived in the land. So, they decided not to cross the Jordan River.

For their unfaithfulness, God decreed that no one in their generation would ever see this promised land except for the other two spies, Joshua and his brother Caleb. For the next forty years, the Israelites walked in a circle around the desert. Then one day, the last person from that generation died, and they no longer traveled in circles. They could head into the Promised Land.

Before Moses died, he put Joshua in charge of leading the Israelites into the Promised Land. Moses encouraged Joshua to be brave and courageous in the land they were going to possess. I believe Moses did this because he wanted Joshua to remember all that God had done for them along the way and not move in fear like the previous generation. He wanted Joshua to be strong and courageous to do what God said to do.

It was the time of year when the river flooded, and God gave them specific instructions about how to cross the Jordan River. God told Joshua to have the priest carry the ark of the covenant in front of all the people. When they arrived at the edge of the Jordan River, the priest was to walk into the river with the Ark of the Covenant. As soon as he walked into the river, the waters stood on edge, and the ground dried up.

The people of Israel crossed the Jordan River while the priest stood in the middle of the river holding the Ark. When everyone had crossed, the priest walked out, and the water began to flow down the Jordan River again. God performed this miracle so that the people would know His mighty power. God also wanted the Israelites to know that He was still with them and would perform mighty miracles like this if they continued to trust in Him.

After they were on the other side, they made camp and waited for God's instructions. This is where we pick up the story of the Israelites in the city of Jericho in the book of Joshua:

Now when Joshua was near Jericho, he looked up and saw a man standing in front of him with a drawn sword in his hand. Joshua went up to him and asked, "Are you for us or for our enemies?"

"Neither," he replied, "but as commander of the army of the LORD I have now come."

Then Joshua fell facedown to the ground in reverence, and asked him, "What message does my Lord have for his servant?"

The commander of the LORD's army replied, "Take off your sandals, for the place where you are standing is holy." And Joshua did so. Now the gates of Jericho were securely barred because of the Israelites. No one went out and no one came in.

Then the LORD said to Joshua, "See, I have delivered Jericho into your hands, along with its king and its fighting men. March around the city once with all the armed men. Do this for six days. Have seven priests carry trumpets of rams' horns in front of the ark. On the seventh day, march around the city seven times, with the priests blowing the trumpets. When you hear them sound a long blast on the trumpets, have the whole army give a loud shout; then the wall of the city will collapse and the army will go up, everyone straight in."

So Joshua son of Nun called the priests and said to them, "Take up the ark of the covenant of the LORD and have seven priests carry trumpets in front of it." And he ordered the army, "Advance! March around the city, with an armed guard going ahead of the ark of the LORD."

When Joshua had spoken to the people, the seven priests carrying the seven trumpets before the LORD went forward, blowing their trumpets, and the ark of the LORD's covenant followed them. The armed guard marched ahead of the priests who blew the trumpets, and the rear guard followed the ark. All this time the trumpets were sounding.

But Joshua had commanded the army, "Do not give a war cry, do not raise your voices, do not say a word until the day I tell you to shout. Then shout!"

So he had the ark of the LORD carried around the city, circling it once. Then the army returned to camp and spent the night there. Joshua got up early the next morning and the priests took up the ark of the LORD. The seven priests carrying the seven trumpets went forward, marching before the ark of the LORD and blowing the trumpets. The armed men went ahead of them and the rear guard followed the ark of the LORD, while the trumpets kept sounding. So on the second day they marched around the city once and returned to the camp. They did this for six days. On the seventh day, they got up at daybreak and marched around the city seven times in the same manner, except that on that day they circled the city seven times.

The seventh time around, when the priests sounded the trumpet blast, Joshua commanded the army, "Shout! For the LORD has given you the city! The city and all that is in it are to be devoted to the LORD. Only Rahab the prostitute and all who are with her in her house shall be spared, because she hid the spies we sent. But keep away from the devoted things, so that you will not bring about your own destruction by taking any of them. Otherwise you will make the camp of Israel liable to destruction and bring trouble on it. All the silver and gold and *the articles of bronze and iron are sacred to the LORD and must go into his treasury."*

When the trumpets sounded, the army shouted, and at the sound of the trumpet, when the men gave a loud shout, the wall collapsed; so everyone charged straight in, and they took the city. They devoted the city to the LORD and destroyed with the sword every living thing in it—men and women, young and old, cattle, sheep and donkeys. Joshua 5:13–6:21

As I read the story of Joshua, I'm hard-pressed to understand how he would have the nerve to instruct his people to do battle in such a way. But Joshua was a man who trusted God, even when he had to do something that no one else would do. The strange things they did were more than unorthodox for any army.

First, Joshua came across a man with a sword who gave Joshua a ridiculous plan for taking the city. When Joshua asked, "Are you for us or our enemies?" he said, "Neither." I am not against you, but I'm not actually for you. And Joshua trusted this man. He fell to the ground in reverence and decided to do what this man, who hadn't pledged allegiance to him, told him to do. Joshua believed the message was from God and had faith that God would give the Israelites a victory.

Next, the Israelites were to walk around the city wall one time each day for six days, not in secret but in broad daylight. They took their most prized and cherished possession—the Ark of the Covenant—and carried it out in the open for the entire enemy army to see while blowing trumpets to announce that they were right outside the city wall. Only God could think up this crazy plan and ask His people to trust Him.

I can't imagine what the people in the city were thinking while all this was happening. They probably were saying to each other, "What kind of weird person put this army up to this?" or "They've spent way too much time in the sun," or "Who would do such a crazy thing?"

On the seventh day, the Israelites were to execute this plan seven times in a row. The entire time, the priest blew the trumpet announcing their presence. Instead of charging the city the seventh time around, the army stood there and yelled in their loudest voices. When they did, the city walls broke apart and fell to the ground. Then, they rushed the city and killed every living thing inside.

Only God would come up with such a crazy plan for His people to capture a city. But that's exactly how God works. Just like He asked Joshua, God asks us to trust Him so much that we let go of our ways of doing things. God wants us to do what NO ONE ELSE DOES, even when we don't know what the result will be. This is ultimate faith in God.

There are stories like Joshua's found throughout the Bible and world history—stories about people who do things that no one else would do that change the world. These are the same people who encourage us to live a life of ultimate freedom and adventure. When we let go of our fears and do what no one else would do, we get to live like no one else lives.

It doesn't matter what others do; what matters is that you do what you know you should do deep down in your heart. Don't try to get everyone's approval or advice, but step out in faith and do that which you are being called to do. Doing things that don't make sense is what changes lives and the world we live in. Doing things that no one else would do isn't easy, but there are things you can do to prepare for such times.

First, I encourage you to read the stories in the Bible and biographies of people who did amazingly unconventional things. Read the stories of risk-takers who stepped out into the unknown and tried what no one else would try. Stories of people like the Wright brothers, who were thought to be crazy because they believed they could fly. Or the life and stories of Harriet Tubman, who was an American slave who gained her freedom. Instead of relishing in this new life, she risked her own life to go back into the slave states to help others gain their freedom as well. Reread the story in the Bible of a shepherd boy who became the king of Israel by taking on a giant with just a few small stones. There are so many stories of people throughout history who moved society forward by thinking differently and not caring that no one else was doing this. By reading these stories of others who risked it all, you'll build the confidence to step out into what you know you should do, even if NO ONE ELSE DOES THIS.

> *It doesn't matter what others do; what matters is that you do what you know you should do deep down in your heart.*

Second, tell your trusted circle of friends what you're going to do. If you don't have a group that is *for* you and that you can trust, then ask God to bring people like that into your life. God wants us to be surrounded by people who are for us. There are countless verses in the Bible about the advantage of having two or three people on your side to encourage you. By surrounding yourself with those people, you'll build the courage to keep going.

And last, don't turn back on the decision you have made—*ever*! People will tell you that what you're doing is stupid, you're out of your mind, or it's not a proper thing to do. That's exactly how the devil works. He puts people in your path who make you question what you're doing to try to get you to turn around. But it doesn't matter what others think or say. They don't answer to God for your life; only you will do that. Live that adventurous life by listening to what God has for you and doing those things that no one else would do.

7

TIMING IS EVERYTHING

I love watching YouTube videos that show people doing crazy things, the really funny ones that highlight other people's foibles—and sometimes their pain. Not that I like to see people get hurt, but seeing other people do unusual things interests me.

One such video was of a group of people on a canoe trip. As they went down the river, they came to an extremely long rope hanging from a tree over the river. They pulled over, and five of them climbed up the bank to take a long swing out over the river. The first guy pulled the rope as tight as he could and leaped off the side of the hill, swinging down and then out over the river. At exactly the right time, he let go of the rope and flew even higher before plunging into the cool water.

The next three each grabbed the rope with gusto and took the swing. But I noticed that the fifth guy was hanging back. After he climbed to the top of the hill, it looked like he was trying to decide if he wanted to take a turn. He was hesitant, and it looked like he might back out and climb back down the hill. But his friends kept yelling for him to grab the rope, swing out over the river, and let go. With every encouragement, he moved closer to stepping out and taking the swing. Then he gripped the rope really hard, tightened every muscle in his entire body, gritted his teeth, and jumped off the ledge.

Just like the others, he started the long swing down toward the water and then the long swing back up as the rope reached its arc. As he came to the pinnacle of the swing, instead of letting go, he held on to the rope and headed back toward the bank with incredible speed. If he didn't let go now, he'd slam into the bank. So, at the bottom of the downward swing, he let go of the rope and smacked hard on the water with jarring force.

His friends showed extreme concern, and then there was a collective grimace as their buddy hit the water. Only when he bobbed back up, having lived through the experience, did they begin to laugh at his misery caused by poor timing. He'd held on too long.

I've seen other videos of people who chose to let go at a different point in the swing. In one of these videos, the rope swing was on the side of a hill, which did *not* start directly over the river. You had to swing out and over a piece of land before you made it to the water.

In one particular video, a young lady seemed hesitant, like the guy I just described. She needed the encouragement of her friends, and they continued to assure her that she could do this. She started and stopped many times, and I wasn't sure she would actually go through with it. But she finally took the leap of faith and jumped out into the unknown for the swing of a lifetime.

Unfortunately, that swing ended far too soon. Before she even reached the edge of the water, she let go and smacked chest-first into the bank of the river. Because of the momentum, when she hit the ground, her entire body and her feet bent backward over her head with so much force that it flipped her over. Seeing this made almost every nerve in my body ring out, as if I'd taken that swing myself. It was painful to watch. The video stopped right after impact, so I never knew the extent of her injuries, but I imagined that for at least the next few weeks she'd be feeling the pain from letting go too soon.

As I think about both these experiences and the incredible pain that came from holding on too long or letting go too soon, I reflect on my life and the times I've held on to things for too long or let go too soon.

Timing is everything.

Perhaps you want to hold on to things that you know you should let go of because you're afraid that when you let go, there will be a negative result. Much of this fear can be erased by letting go only when the time is right. Like on the rope swing, if you let go too late, you could smack down and get hurt. But if you let go too soon, it could be worse.

I'm sure you have questions like these: How will I know when to let go? What if I do this, but it's the wrong time? What if I wait too long? How can I know the proper timing? Let's explore those answers.

Holding On Too Long

When I was trying to determine the appropriate time for Elise to start dating, I initially set strict parameters out of fear: fear of her getting hurt and fear that a pattern could be set that would later be detrimental to her—and even potentially for her marriage. This was very difficult for me. As a father, I wanted what was best for my daughter, and I didn't want her to get hurt. I thought that if I let go of control of this issue too soon, I'd be failing in my responsibility to protect my daughter from the crazy, evil men she knew nothing about. Of course, that sounds like an exaggeration, but that's what I thought.

When God asked me, "When did you dedicate your daughter to Me?" He was teaching me about proper timing. I had to wrestle with my trust in God in the deepest areas of my life. It doesn't hit any harder than with my child.

When Elise approached me wanting something different, she sat on our bed and watched TV with me. She was trying to time her request at just the right point, when I was in a good mood and would hopefully give her the answer she was seeking.

What would have happened if she'd held on too long before asking if she could go to the prom with a date? She knew my strict stance on dating, while at the same time, she had no clue that God had been working on my heart and mind to trust Him with her care. If she hadn't had the courage to approach me that night, the opportunity might not have come up again in time for me to agree with her and meet with the young man who had invited her to prom. It could also have caused issues with their plans and what they wanted to do before and after the dance. It surely would have diminished the enjoyment of what should have been a very fun night.

And for me, what if I'd held on to what I'd always thought was the right time to start dating? What if I hadn't listened to God and had dug in my heels with my belief that the proper timing to date was when a person was ready financially, emotionally, and spiritually—which was not at age sixteen? I could very easily have held on and not let go. And I could very easily have damaged my relationship with Elise. It could have caused a division between us for years to come and caused us unnecessary pain.

Instead, I yielded to what I thought I heard God tell me to do, and I let Him work out the details. By letting go when I felt God's lead, I began the process of building trust in my daughter, which strengthened our relationship and empowered her to make good decisions. At the time, our relationship was on shaky ground because we were both in the process of working through some growth. Looking back, I can see this was an opportunity to let go and trust my daughter to make wise decisions for herself. Later, when I told her that her relationship with JJ looked more like dating than friendship, it showed that I trusted her and was willing to stand by her decision to date someone she really liked. But if I had stood my ground and been unwilling to let go, I could have pushed my daughter further away from me, destroying the relationship I was trying to build.

It was an incredible honor when Elise asked me to type the message to JJ about meeting with me before they had permission to date, and it made this moment even more special. Holding on to my control too long would have taken this moment away.

Good timing was also a factor when Laura and I decided to sell our house, and things didn't happen overnight. One day we each thought, *I don't know if I'm attached to this house anymore,* not knowing the other one was thinking the same thing. For the next year and a half, we tried to decide if we should sell.

Later, when I rode horses with my friend, John, and asked him if it was a good time to sell, I surprised myself. I had no intention of asking him that question. And I wasn't expecting him to give me the advice that you sometimes need to step out in faith, let go of what you're clinging to, and let God move for you.

I told Laura about that conversation and said that I wondered if selling was something we should do at that time. Were we holding on to something that God wanted us to let go of? And how could we know when the perfect time was?

I don't know what it was about that event that made us decide to sell the house that day, but I do know that we both felt that we needed to take this step of faith and see what God would do. Maybe the perfect time was simply when we felt God prompt us to move. If we held on to the house, it wasn't a sin, but it would have blocked our next year of growth. We could have missed the opportunity to deepen our trust and faith in God, to let Him move on our behalf.

> *Maybe the perfect time was simply when we felt God prompt us to move.*

Over the next few weeks, we prepared to sell the house, and it was a very nerve-racking time for me. Additionally, Laura and I weren't seeing eye-to-eye in our marriage, which was uncommon for us. I struggled in prayer every morning, wanting to hear God say, "Thus saith moveth," but that voice never came. All I heard Him say was, "Be patient in the process." This wasn't what I wanted to hear, but it was what I needed to hear. It confirmed that this was the right time to let go and see what God would do.

If we hadn't let go at that time, we wouldn't have experienced so many things that happened afterward. We would have missed out on seeing God move in ways that we wouldn't have expected, which drew us closer to God as individuals and as a family.

Because we didn't hold on too long, God began speaking in a deeper way to both of us. Or maybe our ears started hearing Him more clearly because we'd placed ourselves in a position where we needed Him. During the sale of the house, we both picked up on things that people said, directly or indirectly, and we knew that only God could have had us hear those things at that time. The timing was perfect because we moved when we felt God telling us to move.

When Laura and I began to look around for apartments, we found a brand-new complex that had just been built. It had a beautiful pool, a fitness center, a dog park (we had a dog at the time), and beautiful green spaces. And we would be the first ones to move into the newly built apartment. We then decided to rent two units next door to each other to have extra space for guests and for Elise when she came home. It gave her a place to stay during the COVID-19 lockdown when colleges sent the students home.

Yes, our house had been the perfect place for a specific season of life when we were raising our family. But holding on to it too long could have taken away the things that we needed to grow in our relationship with both God and each other. The apartments brought us closer together in a very odd way that we never expected.

Letting Go Too Soon

When Laura and I first began talking about selling the house in the fall of 2017, if we'd done so right away instead of waiting two years, we would have been letting go too soon and could have brought unnecessary pain to all of us. We needed that time to get comfortable with the idea, and we needed that time for the house to fulfill its purpose for our family.

In the fall of 2017, Elise started college a short twenty-minute drive from our house. And even though she was close to home, she was out on her own and learning to manage her life. She had to define what she believed for herself then live out those beliefs, and having a familiar, stable place to come back to helped her through this transition. If we'd acted too fast, we would have taken away that anchor.

At the same time, Raquel was entering high school, which can be some of the hardest years of a young person's life. The school she attended was going through many changes that impacted the students because of new leadership at the top level. This resulted in changes at the school and how it was run.

There were things that Raquel had hoped to do in high school, like be on the dance team. After being on the dance team her freshman year, the athletic department went through some drastic changes, and they dropped the ball in some areas, like bringing in a new dance coach. After her freshman year, the dance team was dismantled—a grave disappointment for Raquel.

At the same time, her youth leader decided to move back to Norway with his wife and family. He'd been a very important influence in her life and had helped her find answers about her belief in Jesus. Losing him was another blow.

Since we didn't decide to move in 2017, both our girls were able to come home to a familiar, safe home. It offered them stability, a place where they could breathe and take a break from the things that troubled them. It was a place of security and familiarity.

Furthermore, if we'd let go of the house too soon, our apartment complex wouldn't have been built yet. Of course, there are always other apartments, but for us and the transition we went through, this complex was perfectly located and had all the amenities we wanted that made the move much easier.

During that same time, our company was just around the corner from making some big changes as my brothers and I tried to figure out whether to sell the company or bring in new leadership. Just two years earlier, each of us had said that we wanted to find someone who could eventually replace us and run our area of the company.

There was so much work to be done, and the systems and processes we had in place at the time couldn't support the growth. And some of the leaders we had in place didn't have the skill set or capacity to take the company to the next level. Bringing in the third generation a couple of years later allowed us each to move in a new direction where God was taking us. It wasn't an easy transition, but looking back, we all agree that the timing was perfect.

If we'd let go of our leadership roles too soon—in 2015, when we first had the discussion—I'm convinced this would have caused us incredible pain as a company and could have ruined everything we'd worked for up to that point. We needed to wait for the right timing in order to get the right people in leadership.

In the fall of 2017, it was time for each of my brothers and me to take flight into what God had for each of us, and we made the decision to let go. It was not too soon, and it was not too late. The timing was perfect, and God was gracious to each of us.

King Solomon is thought to be the wisest person who ever lived. When he became king of Israel, he had a dream one night. In 1 Kings 3:5, it says, "At Gibeon the Lord appeared to Solomon during the night in a dream, and God said, 'Ask for whatever you want me to give you.'" And in verse nine, Solomon responded by saying, "So give your servant a discerning heart to govern your people and to distinguish between right and wrong. For who is able to govern this great people of yours?" God responds in verse twelve when He says, "I will do what you have asked. I will give you a wise and discerning heart, so that there will never have been anyone like you, nor will there ever be."

Solomon received a discerning heart from God because he asked for it. With a discerning heart, we can also have the wisdom to know the perfect time to let go of that which we know we should let go of.

Solomon wrote down the wisdom he received, which can be found in several books in the Old Testament. In the book of Ecclesiastes, he gives advice about the seasons and timing of what we experience in life. Verses one through eight say this:

There is a time for everything,
and a season for every activity under the heavens:
a time to be born and a time to die,
a time to plant and a time to uproot,
a time to kill and a time to heal,
a time to tear down and a time to build,
a time to weep and a time to laugh,
a time to mourn and a time to dance,
a time to scatter stones and a time to gather them,
a time to embrace and a time to refrain from embracing,
a time to search and a time to give up,
a time to keep and a time to throw away,
a time to tear and a time to mend,
a time to be silent and a time to speak,
a time to love and a time to hate,
a time for war and a time for peace.

When I read these verses, it helps me understand that God directs everything in our lives. Yet there's a perfect timing for them to take place. This passage indicates that there are only two things where we cannot choose the timing—the time to be born and the time to die. Everything else is a choice, and we get to decide when they will take place. And when we wonder how we can know the right timing, Solomon gives us the answer to that question when he was told by God in his dream, "Ask for whatever you want me to give you." We go to God and ask Him for the wisdom to make decisions. And like Solomon, when we ask for something that God also desires in us—like wisdom—God will give us what we ask.

In Ecclesiastes 3:9–11, Solomon continues with more wisdom on the proper timing:

> *What do workers gain from their toil?*
> *I have seen the burden God has laid on the human race.*
> *He has made everything beautiful in its time.*
> *He has also set eternity in the human heart; yet no one can*
> *fathom what God has done from beginning to end.*

Solomon writes that He has made everything beautiful in its time. If we try to rush things, we create a burden we have to manage. But when we wait for God's timing, God alone carries the burden. God sets the perfect time for us in all situations, and we can know that perfect timing by listening to Him and moving only when we hear Him prompt us to move.

If we try to rush things, we create a burden we have to manage. But when we wait for God's timing, God alone carries the burden.

Though we cannot fathom what God has done, He has set the timing of all things in our hearts. Eternity encompasses all things, and God will give us this perfect timing if we will wait and be patient for Him to prompt us to move at precisely the right time.

My friend Mark once pointed out something interesting that he found when looking at verses two through four. Instead of reading horizontally from left to right, he read these verses vertically. This is what he saw:

*a time to be **born***	*a time to **die,***
*a time to **plant***	*a time to **uproot,***
*a time to **kill***	*a time to **heal,***
*a time to **tear down***	*a time to **build,***
*a time to **weep***	*a time to **laugh,***
*a time to **mourn***	*a time to **dance,***

There's a time to be born, plant, kill, tear down, weep, and mourn. However, there's also a time to die (die to your ways), uproot (uproot your way of thinking), heal (heal what has hurt you), build (build on what God has for you), laugh (laugh with a new joy in life) and dance (dance because of what's changed in you).

When I read it like this, I saw some areas in my life where I needed to let go, so I could get from the point of dying to holding on, to dancing because I'd learned to let go. I now find pleasure in seeking God's perfect timing rather than stressing over when that time should be. I've learned that God's timing is perfect.

I now find pleasure in seeking God's perfect timing rather than stressing over when that time should be. I've learned that God's timing is perfect.

141

There are many other great verses that speak of God's perfect timing that have helped me over the years. I would suggest that to know God's perfect timing, it's good to study verses like these:

Proverbs 3:5–6
Trust in the LORD **with all your heart**
 and lean not on your own understanding;
in all your ways submit to him,
 and he will make your paths straight.

Jeremiah 29:11–12
"For I know the plans I have for you," declares the Lord, "plans to prosper you and not to harm you, plans to give you hope and a future. Then you will call on me and come and pray to me, and I will listen to you."

Proverbs 16:9
In their hearts humans plan their course,
 but the Lord **establishes their steps.**

Proverbs 27:1
Do not boast about tomorrow, for you do not know what a day may bring.

You don't want to get ahead of God, and you don't want to sit when you should move. Be patient in all your decisions because God's timing is perfect. When you have a sensitive heart like Solomon to wait upon God, He will always show you the right time to let go.

As you begin to let go of those things you don't need anymore, your understanding of what God wants from you becomes clearer. Learn to listen to God for the right timing, then act. Change is hard, but if we embrace it early, it makes the transition so much easier.

People often ask me how to hear from God. I tell them to trust the voice they hear in their head (the positive one). Most of the time, God's voice sounds like our voice in our head. The more we learn to trust this voice, the faster we'll be able to let go of what we don't need.

Isaiah 30:21 says, "Whether you turn to the right or to the left, your ears will hear a voice behind you, saying, 'This is the way; walk in it.'" When we have a relationship with God and walk according to His ways, the voice we hear is His Holy Spirit. To determine if it is God's voice, ask yourself if the message aligns with God's Word and if it is for your benefit. As Jeremiah 29:11 states, "His plan is to prosper us and not harm us."

Learn to be more patient, die to having to have your way now, and be open to change. When we aren't patient to wait for the perfect timing, it causes all kinds of anxiety. By waiting on God's timing, you'll find peace in the transition. That doesn't mean it will be easy, but you'll be at peace because you haven't rushed into something you aren't sure of. You will be at rest that God will provide for you.

What can you do while you're waiting on God? Research and study. This is a time to uproot old ways of thinking or build the future for those things that will help you when it's time to let go. By researching what the next step may be or studying about the next chapter of your life, you'll be more prepared to step into it. You'll be able to see the timing more clearly.

I like to get away to read my Bible and pray. I ask God for direction in the timing and to show me those stories or passages that will guide me in patience and lead me to the proper timing for the decisions I need to make. Every time I go to God, He gives me a clear direction through His Word—if I'm patient enough to wait for His answer. While you're waiting on God, get away for a few days in solitude with just yourself and God. His will is always to be found when you seek Him.

Don't feel like you must move right away in any situation. Take the time to reflect on where you are. This can be a time of healing and preparing for when you let go. By slowing down and waiting on God's timing, you'll be able to reflect on what the past has taught you, where you are in the present, and how the future will look.

8

I'M AFRAID OF FAILING

In the mid-seventies, my parents began attending a nonde-nominational church in the Saint Louis area. During one of the meetings, as my parents listened to the Word, they felt the pull to follow Jesus. That night, our entire family went forward together and made the decision to follow Jesus. This one act of faith changed the course of our entire family for the rest of our lives.

For years, my parents sat in church and listened to stories from different missionaries who spoke at the church. The more they listened, the more they felt pulled to go to other countries themselves and tell about how Jesus had changed their lives. But how could they do this? My father was a barber, and he had to work every day to make a living. He didn't have the financial resources to pick up and leave for the mission field. Nor did he feel it was right to depend on the generosity of others to provide for them on the mission field. Instead, he had a strong feeling that God would finance their mission through some sort of business venture that would fund their needs. Then a man who sold my father hair-care products told him that the owner of his company might be willing to sell his distributorship. My father was interested because he thought it might be a way to release them into the mission field.

Moving in this direction required my parents to let go of a very secure source of income, learn how to manage a sales team, and basically put everything on the line that they'd worked for up to that point. If they let go of this security, there was no turning back. My father had such a great reputation in the community that when he sold his barbershop, he had to sign a non-compete agreement to not open another one in that same area for five years. Because my parents had let go of my dad's profession and set out to pursue their dream, they knew they couldn't fail at this new venture.

On October 31, 1980, my dad and mom stepped out into the unknown, hoping this new venture would eventually provide the money they needed to go to the mission field. They not only sold the barbershop, but they also sold a duplex that had provided a monthly income, and they took out a loan on their house. It was a big step, and there was no guarantee of success.

Within a few weeks, Dad found out that the previous owner hadn't disclosed all the financial information. Money was owed to vendors, and there were undisclosed issues with the inventory that my parents assumed. This created so much stress that my parents wondered if they'd really heard from God. I remember the many loud phone calls Dad had with the previous owner, explaining what he'd found and asking how the former owner would rectify this. Unfortunately, my parents had bought the company and everything that went with it, including the debts.

Every morning when I came downstairs to go to school, I saw my mom and dad on their knees in our living room, praying that God would keep them from losing everything that they'd invested in. When they finished praying at our house, they went to work early and spent at least another hour praying over the company before they began their business day.

Being able to let go of something secure and step into something so uncertain could have only been done because they had faith that God would provide for them and that He had directed them to buy the company. However, this didn't mean they didn't have to face the fear of failure. As a matter of fact, my parents faced this fear every day they owned the business. They lived day by day, just trying to make ends meet. Their fear of failure was only eliminated by their trust and faith in God.

The business that they'd acquired sold beauty-care products to beauty shops and also rented shampoo systems to them. These shampoo systems were comprised of an air compressor attached to a five-gallon metal tank that held diluted shampoo. A hose ran from the tank to the shampoo bowl, where clients got their hair washed. The idea was to eliminate all the extra bottles in a beauty shop.

One day in 1984, a dog groomer went to get her hair done at a local beauty shop. She thought this shampoo system would be

> *They lived day by day, just trying to make ends meet. Their fear of failure was only eliminated by their trust and faith in God.*

perfect in her dog grooming shop. It could eliminate much of the wasted shampoo that occurs while washing a dog.

She called my father and asked if she could have one installed. Because he needed any money he could get, he kindly agreed to let her rent one. She, in turn, told others, and within the next few years, we began renting these shampoo systems to more and more dog groomers.

Then we thought of selling a pet shampoo that could be used with these systems. By 1988, we had closed down the beauty end of the business and moved everything into my parents' basement. My dad and my oldest brother, Don, began trading weeks where they would travel, install these shampoo systems, and sell shampoo.

In 1990, we rented a 2,500 square foot warehouse, so we could make the shampoos ourselves. The company was now going full time into the dog shampoo business, and I'd graduated high school and was selling all the shampoo I could.

Many years after the company started prospering and started a trajectory of growth, my father said something that helped me understand why his fear of failure had been so strong. It helped me understand the pressure he felt and why it was so important for him to know that every move he made was because he was following what God intended. For the first time, he shared a story of generational failures that preceded him.

My parents, my brothers, and I had met for prayer on a Monday morning before work like we'd done so many Monday mornings before. After we prayed, we discussed a major opportunity before us that came with some major investment risk.

It wasn't much different from other opportunities that we'd looked at in the past, but for some reason, this one triggered a memory in my father's mind that he shared with the rest of us. He said that up until this time in our extended family, my parents' move to take a major risk was the only one that had been a success. He went on to tell us the stories of other family members who'd risked it all and failed.

Dad's great-grandfather had started a company, and not too many years after he was in business, the company failed. So, he went back to work for another company. His grandfather had also tried to branch out on his own without success. Finally, his father let go of everything to start his own company, but this company also failed. His dad went on to be a very successful executive in a local retail chain, but his dream of owning his own company never materialized. After telling us the stories of the previous generations, my father strongly cautioned us to be careful about taking on more than we could handle. He didn't say not to do what we were discussing; he just shared these stories as a warning against thinking that things would always go our way.

These stories stuck with me. They provide a warning that's always in my mind when I'm making a big decision—a warning to carefully think through the decision. However, I've also learned not to let a fear of failure control my decisions. I learn from the past, but I don't let the past control me.

My parents never let fear of failure control them either, but that didn't mean it didn't whisper in their ears and try to take over their minds. In fact, almost everything my parents did in both business and ministry came with a great risk of failure.

But when it was time to let go of the security they had and risk failure, they chose to be on the side of God, not the inner fear that could have easily controlled them if they let it.

My parents never let fear of failure control them either, but that didn't mean it didn't whisper in their ears and try to take over their minds.

Today, the company that they risked everything for has grown into a worldwide entity that sells products to more than seventy countries and employs over three hundred people. They also started a nonprofit organization that serves the needs of the poor and needy around the world called Gifts of Love International, and they've realized their dream of being worldwide missionaries. Rather than fearing the failures of past family members, they trusted that God would lead them to success.

In 2017, our company was growing at a very fast pace. Since 2009, we'd enjoyed a growth rate of 20 percent or more year over year. A dental brand that we launched had grown to be the leading dental brand for dogs internationally. Major retailers both in the US and around the world gave us retail space on shelves that were once held for other, more prominent branded companies' products.

The success was both a blessing from God, but it also became a greater burden on my brothers and me. As I shared in earlier chapters, I wanted to let go of my leadership responsibilities, but I didn't want to risk the failure of putting the wrong person in charge.

As we began to talk more about who would lead the company, the fear of failing at this transition grew inside me. I thought back to what my father had said about the previous generations and wondered if that would happen to us. Were we making the wrong move at the wrong time?

In a very short six months, my brothers and I had stepped away as leaders and turned everything over to the next generation. For the first time, other people were making the directional decisions we'd always made.

Every time the fear of failing rose in me, I thought, *Look at the change as an opportunity to step toward where God is leading you and trust God for the result.* When I viewed the decision as an opportunity to step into my purpose, it helped me understand that the decision wasn't final; it was a decision to do things differently than they'd been done before. If it didn't work out, it wasn't a failure but another opportunity to make a change.

In 2018, our new leadership implemented many changes. Employees who had been with us for a very long time decided to pursue other employment opportunities. We hired others to replace them or moved people around to fill these many roles. We hired more employees that year than we'd ever hired in any year before. At the same time, we were also changing IT systems. It was a challenge to implement new systems while trying to teach all the employees how to use them. I was probably one of the slowest ones to learn, and it became very frustrating for me. We also changed from using Mac computers to PCs, and although we joked about it, this was very difficult for my brothers and me.

I had spent over twenty-eight years building the sales organization of the company. I knew almost every customer and had visited nearly 90 percent of their businesses. Our relationships were not just business; they were personal. My fear of letting those people down was acute. I was afraid that my letting go could cause a failure in their businesses because they'd focused on our products. If the relationship wasn't well maintained, it could translate into a failure for us—and them as well.

If it didn't work out, it wasn't a failure but another opportunity to make a change.

Toward the end of 2018, I noticed that sales were no longer on the same trajectory as the previous many years. It looked like we'd only recognize a 2 to 4 percent growth that year rather than our normal 20 percent. I began to wonder if I'd made the right decision.

In February 2019, we had our first board meeting of the year. During this meeting, Landon, our CEO, presented all the 2018 reports. He said that we'd grown 3 percent that year. I wasn't surprised because we track sales growth in real time, and I'd been following it. I was surprised that the growth rate was so low, especially after making so many beneficial changes. And then Landon discussed our debt. In 2018, we'd paid off almost every loan we had—into the millions of dollars. To pay off all our loans, hire all the people we did, and still grow 3 percent was absolutely incredible. The change hadn't been a failure at all. In fact, it was a roaring success.

The fear of failure isn't anything new. The Bible is rich with stories about people who had to release their fears to achieve the success God had in store for them. They, too, weren't certain they were making the right decisions, but they chose to trust God to determine their steps.

When Moses led his people out of slavery in Egypt, his plan was fraught with opportunities to fail. He told the Israelites that they'd defeat the Egyptians by allowing God to move on their behalf. God would send ten plagues on the Egyptians, and then the Pharaoh would ask them to leave. The Israelites trusted Moses enough that they did everything he asked them to do. This included each family killing a lamb and smearing the blood over the doorpost of their house. What leader would suggest that? The one who is *not* led by the fear of failure!

Before Pharoah asked the Israelites to leave Egypt, Moses told them to plunder the Egyptians—the very ones who'd enslaved them. The Bible says in Exodus 3:22, "Every woman is to ask her neighbor and any woman living in her house for articles of silver and gold and for clothing, which you will put on your sons and daughters. And so, you will plunder the Egyptians." This could have gone totally wrong, and it almost did. The Israelites were chased to the Red Sea with the Egyptians hot on their trail. Then at the last moment, God parted the water, the Israelites crossed to the other shore, and they were saved. Then the sea returned to its natural state, drowning many of the Egyptians who pursued them.

Moses and the Israelites are just like us—fragile human beings. The only difference is they didn't let their inner fear of failure grow larger than their inner faith in God. They had

153

been captive for over four hundred years, but they chose to follow what God had in store for them. The result was freedom from slavery. I think they made the right choice.

The Bible tells us that Jesus came as a baby, born in a manger to regular people. He didn't come as a son of a king. He was not even born into a prominent family. He was just a baby born to a woman who was a virgin and a man who made a living by building furniture.

Moses and the Israelites are just like us—fragile human beings. The only difference is they didn't let their inner fear of failure grow larger than their inner faith in God.

As Jesus grew up, He learned his father's trade while also studying the Jewish religion, as all good Jewish boys did. At twelve, He went through the process in the Jewish culture of becoming a man, and we don't know much more about Him until we pick up His life story when He was thirty.

He was baptized by John the Baptist, who baptized many people in that region. When he baptized Jesus, the heavens opened, and a voice pronounced, "This is my son, whom I love; with him, I am well pleased" (Mathew 3:17). Then the Spirit of God came down and rested upon Jesus. Many believe this was the start of His ministry.

We pick up the life of Jesus when He goes out and chooses twelve men who decide to let go of their life to follow Him. Surely, they each had an inner fear of failure at the beginning of this journey. They needed the teaching and the training that Jesus provided to increase their faith in Him and the plan that God had for them. We know this is true because, throughout the book of Matthew, Jesus refers to them as people of little faith. If Jesus addressed their lack of faith, he was also addressing their inner fear of failure.

Jesus was arrested and tried as a criminal, then crucified on a Roman cross. The twelve men who'd been following Him were filled with inner fear, and they hid from the Roman soldiers and the Jewish leaders. Peter, the one who Jesus said would build his church, denied that he knew Jesus three times to a little girl. The others went into hiding; two took off running from Jerusalem. But these were the special people Jesus had chosen to follow Him. He must have known something we didn't.

On the third day, the Bible tells us that Jesus rose from the grave. He was first seen by the two who had run seven miles from Jerusalem. After He revealed himself to them, they ran back to tell the others. As soon as they arrived, Jesus walked into the room to prove that He was actually alive. Though physically alive, He also had a glorified body that still showed the marks where the nails had been pounded through His wrists.

Jesus spent the next forty days with these disciples, teaching them and encouraging their faith in Him. Then at the end of the forty days, He went to a mountain and was taken into heaven in a cloud. Before He went away, He told them that through them (these same men who had hidden because of their fear of failure), He would change the world.

If anyone should have had a fear of failure, it should have been Jesus. He turned over the entire plan to change the world to this ragtag group of men. When they did what he told them to do—"Wait for the gift my Father promised" (Acts

1:4)—they received the Holy Spirit as their counselor and were given the faith to believe that they could do what Jesus told them they *could* do.

Jesus didn't need to include these twelve disciples. God created the entire Universe in six days, and Jesus could have easily fixed all the problems of the world in the forty days after His resurrection. But He didn't do that. His plan was to use messed-up people like the disciples (people like you and me) to change this world. We all have an inner fear of failure from time to time because of many things in our life, including our past failures, but just like the disciples, we can't let our past determine the good that God has for us. We plan our course and trust God to determine the steps that we take, then we let go of our fear of failure and trust in those steps.

> *Just like the disciples, we can't let our past determine the good that God has for us.*

Our past doesn't determine our future. Instead, it allows us to learn how we can live our life differently. Both Moses and the disciples let go of the failures of their past to press on to that goal that God had given them. It wasn't that they didn't remember the past failures—they probably were reminded of them often. They just made up their minds not to let these past failures determine their future success.

The Process

Consider each decision to let go as an opportunity to change and reach your purpose in life. Making the decision to let go is not finality; it's the opportunity to do things differently than you've done before. Later—if you need to—you can always make another decision.

Here's what I suggest: Get a piece of paper and write down the positive results of letting go of this situation or thing. By writing down the positive results in detail, you'll see that failure is just a fear, not a reality. Fear has been said to be *False Evidence Appearing Real*. When you recognize that, your fear will no longer dictate your decision to let go. Define each positive aspect of letting go, then list people who are *for you* in your decision. When you define the positive aspects of the decision, the ones that looked like failure begin to no longer appear so large. The people on your list will be the ones to cheer you on to your success.

When you stop considering past decisions as failures, you'll be free to focus only on what leads you to success. You'll begin to see what you learned from those earlier painful decisions. When you realize that in your weakness you find strength in God, then you can find peace because you'll know that you aren't good enough on your own anyway.

Let go of your fear of failure. What you're trying to hold on to will eventually pass anyway. We all eventually die at some point, so hold loosely to what you're going for in life and the fears you have along the way. This will bring you peace because just as what you're letting go of was not for eternity, what you're stepping into will also end or be carried on by others.

9

TIME TO CHOOSE

In 2015, my two daughters were attending a local Christian school. Every Thursday before school, they had a chapel service, and the school invited guest speakers to address the student body. I attended these chapels many times because I enjoyed hearing the speaker's personal stories.

One Thursday morning, the school invited a local pastor to speak. To this day, I don't remember his name (I'll call him Bob) or what church he served in—but I'll never forget the story he told and the impact it had on me. His message not only changed my life, but it would become an integral part of what happened in my life, and it's what inspired me to write this book. His story helped me make one of the hardest yet most important decisions—a decision about letting go that changed my life forever.

Bob had an awful temper when he was younger. He got furious at the most trivial things. He didn't even care that he was such an angry person; he simply felt that the only way to get his point across was with anger. He enjoyed a good argument or fight, and sometimes he'd pick a fight for no reason.

One day, his neighbor parked on the street in front of Bob's house. Parking was very tight in that neighborhood, and it was always hard to find a spot. However, there was an unwritten rule that you parked in front of your own house. On this day, someone else had parked in front of his neighbor's house, so the neighbor parked in front of Bob's house.

That day was already not going well for Bob. When he finally arrived home, he saw the neighbor's car parked in front of his house. Immediately, he slammed his hand into the steering wheel and began cussing. He couldn't believe that the neighbor had the nerve to park in his spot. He went on to park his car three more houses down the street.

Bob began his short walk home, but by this time, he was fuming and couldn't let the situation go. He had to address this, and he had to address it now! When he got to his neighbor's house, he began banging on the door. When the man opened the door, Bob let go and gave him a severe tongue lashing.

Unfortunately, Bob's neighbor could also get very angry very easily, and he screamed back at Bob with his side of the story. Soon, they were in the front yard, ready to fight. Bob, being much smaller than his neighbor, continued to yell about the offense but walked toward his house in a rage.

As soon as he went inside, he went to his father's room and grabbed the pistol from the nightstand next to his bed. He loaded it with two bullets, pulled back the trigger, aimed the gun at his neighbor's house, and pulled the trigger twice.

BANG! BANG! He fired two shots from inside his house toward his neighbor's house.

This made Bob feel much better. He knew his neighbor would get the point to never take his parking spot again. Of course, now there were two holes in the wall, so Bob took two pictures and hung them over the holes. He was satisfied that he'd won the war over the parking spot.

The next day when Bob arrived home, he noticed that someone else had parked in his spot again. This time it was a police car, and there was an ambulance in front of his neighbor's house. Bob found another place to park, walked back to his house, and went inside with no concern about what was happening with the neighbors. A few minutes later, there was a knock at the door. It was a policeman, wanting to speak with whoever lived there.

"My family and I live here," Bob said.

The police officer said, "We got a call from your neighbor's work when he didn't show up today. They asked us to stop in and check on him because he never misses work, and they were worried. When we entered the house, we found that your neighbor had been shot and killed. It looks like it probably happened yesterday around this same time. Did you happen to hear or see anything out of the ordinary yesterday?"

When Bob heard this, he got very scared, and a big lump formed in his throat. But he said, "No, I didn't hear or see anything."

After a few more simple questions, the police officer asked Bob to call him right away if he remembered anything or heard something about the shooting.

Bob was worried that he would get caught for this, but that never happened. The detectives investigated the case for many months but never got any leads. Bob always wondered if his two bullets had hit his neighbor or if his death was just a coincidence. After a long while, the detectives moved on to other cases, and Bob and his family eventually moved from the area.

Bob went on to college, got married, and had children. He also went on to change his life by accepting Jesus Christ as his Savior and asking God to forgive all the sins of his past. He then went on to get his theology degree, and he served in his local church as a youth pastor. Bob's past was in his past, and he thought about it less and less over the years until he eventually forgot about it altogether.

Around the time that Bob turned forty, life was very good for him. He and his wife were deeply in love, and his children were growing to be really good kids. Bob and his wife loved the people around them and served in any way they could. Bob had become the lead youth pastor at a very large church in the city where he lived. Life had definitely changed for Bob. Even the temper he once had was no longer a factor in his life. He was so thankful to God for all that He'd done for him and the life he was living.

One morning before he began his day, Bob was praying just like he'd done for years. He thanked God for all His kindness and prayed for others who needed prayer. Then he felt God ask a question that made Bob pause and reflect on the answer.

"Am I the Lord of your life?"

Bob quickly replied aloud to the question, "Yes, of course, You're the Lord of my life. I love You so much, and I wouldn't be in the place I am in life except for You doing all this for me."

Again, Bob felt God ask, "Yes, but do you trust Me as Lord of your life over everything?"

Bob paused at the question being asked again, then replied, "I trust You with everything in my life. Yes, You are the Lord of everything I am or have."

Suddenly, a memory from long ago came back to Bob's mind. It was when he was younger and shot the gun at his neighbor's house. Almost immediately, he felt God ask a question again.

"Am I the Lord of your life, even when you shot the gun at your neighbor's house?"

All the emotion of what Bob had done in the past came rushing forward. He'd never addressed the incident. He began to think hard about what was being asked of him, and eventually, with a quiver in his voice, he replied, "Yes, You are Lord, even of that time. I know You've forgiven me, and my life has changed because of Your forgiveness. You are first in everything in my life."

Then Bob felt God say, "If I'm truly the Lord of your life and you fully trust Me, you must tell the police what you've done. Trust Me as Lord to take care of you, no matter the outcome."

Bob began to cry, overwhelmed with what was being asked of him. Yes, he trusted God with everything in his life, but this was so much to ask. Because of the potential outcome, he began questioning if he'd heard God correctly, wondering if it was guilt that had come back to haunt him.

Again, he heard, "If I'm truly the Lord of your life and you fully trust Me, you need to tell the police what you've done. Trust Me as Lord to take care of you, no matter what."

Bob felt he needed to take some time to think deeply about the choice before him. Did he truly trust God as the Lord of his life? A week passed, and he continued to think and pray about it. Would he trust God with everything—even his past?

Bob decided that he had no other choice. He would trust God with whatever came from confessing what he'd done, something that was known only to him and God. If this went bad for him, he could lose everything he'd worked so hard to build in his life. He could get a long prison sentence, possibly lose his family, his job, and any life that he'd once dreamed of. But Bob committed to putting his full faith and trust that God had the best for him, even if it meant years in prison.

The first thing he did was pull his family together and tell them the entire story of what he'd done and what God had asked him to do. He told them that things could possibly go very badly for him, but he needed to make this choice to trust God as not only his Savior but the Lord of his life as well. It was a very emotional meeting, and there was much discussion to make sure Bob had clearly heard what was being asked of him.

His next step was to seek the support of the church in his decision. He asked for a meeting with the lead pastor of the church where he served. A few hours later, he was in front of that pastor.

Bob said, "I need to tell you about something from my past, and I'm asking you to stand with me in my decision."

The pastor replied, "Bob, you can tell me anything. We, of course, will stand with you. And everything is confidential, except murder."

Bob's face turned a pale white, and he told the entire story of what he'd done and what God was asking him to do. He finished by saying, "I've already made the decision to tell the police. Would you stand with me in this and go with me when I confess what I did?"

The lead pastor was absolutely amazed by all that Bob told him and his willingness to trust God with everything and put his entire life in God's hands. He replied, "Of course, the church will stand with you, and I will go with you to talk with the police."

Bob already had a lawyer lined up to meet with him and his pastor when they arrived at the police station. They entered and sat in front of a detective and an aide to the district attorney. He began by telling them why he was there and then told the story from his past. After a few questions by the detective, Bob was handcuffed and taken in back to the jail. He'd already arranged everything and bonded out of jail that night to await his fate.

Over the next few weeks, Bob, his family and friends, and many people from church prayed earnestly for Bob. He was very clear that he didn't want them praying from a place of fear of the future but from a place of *hope* that God would take care of him no matter what the D.A. decided.

Eventually, he got a call from his lawyer that the D.A. was ready to speak with them. Bob went to the meeting with his lawyer and his pastor.

The D.A. looked frazzled and very tired when he said, "We want to thank you for your honesty and for coming in and telling us what you've done. We've spent the last few weeks looking into your story and pulling together old evidence from the case. After reviewing both your story and the evidence, we see that the two line up perfectly, and we believe that your neighbor died as the result of you pulling the trigger that day."

"As we reviewed the case and looked at all the evidence, we believe we have a case for either murder or manslaughter. With either of these charges, the minimum sentence would be ten years in prison if you're found guilty."

Bob's heart sank when he heard this, yet his spirit was strong. He'd made his choice to *trust God fully*, and he knew that God would take care of him, even if it meant prison time. However, what the D.A. said next totally shocked both Bob and the others.

"I have a problem, though," he said. "There are two major cases in our city that have garnered national news, and our court system is overwhelmed. I don't think we could give this case the proper time, and we wouldn't be able to bring it to trial for many years. Because you came in and told us everything, we don't feel it would be a fair and swift trial. We're going to close the case, never to be opened again. You are free to go."

With that, the D.A. stood up, shook Bob's and his lawyer's hand, and left the room. Bob completely lost it after the D.A. left. He cried tears of joy and thankfulness to God for what had just happened. He couldn't believe that his choice to let go of his past and to trust God, no matter the consequence, could have turned out as it did. Bob was a free man.

Bob didn't tell us how many years ago that had taken place, but it had a tremendous impact on me. He challenged the student body and me (since I was in the audience) with this question: "If faced with the choice to reveal the hidden things in your past, would you trust God as the Lord of your life, no matter the consequence? Are you willing to step into a life of fully trusting God as your Lord and Savior?"

My Choice

It had now been four years since I heard Bob tell his story. Ever since then, I'd always wondered if I trusted God as Lord of my life like Bob did.

In 2019, Laura and I were experiencing many changes in our lives. Elise was now in college, Raquel was in high school, and I'd fully turned over my role in the company to other people. Laura and I were trying to figure out what we would do with our lives and how we could serve in the church.

I truly felt that my walk with God was strong and that He had opened opportunities for me over the past few years that I could never have imagined. It seemed like He was constantly revealing new things to me and wanted to use me in some mighty way that I couldn't quite put my finger on.

At the same time, our marriage was struggling. I was always good at putting on the face that life was grand, but on the inside, I was really struggling with both my future and joy in my marriage. I tried to look the part of having it all together, but I felt I was falling apart.

I had the habit of waking up early and taking time to read the Bible and pray. During one of these devotion times, I felt God speak something to my spirit. When He said it, I was both excited and fearful at the same time. He was speaking to me about our marriage.

I heard, "The middle of 2019 will be one of the hardest times you've ever gone through, but you'll come out of 2019 with a brand-new freedom."

So many thoughts went through my head. Because our marriage was struggling, I wondered if there could be a possibility that Laura and I wouldn't be together at the end of the year. We'd been fighting a lot, and I couldn't see how this would change.

From time to time, I wondered what God's message meant. At other times, I didn't give it much thought. We just went on living life and trying to figure out how we would give of ourselves now that life was changing—though this was much more a question that I struggled with than Laura.

In May of that year, we'd sold the horses, and in June, we decided to put the house up for sale. I don't remember the fight that Laura and I had in June, but it was so severe that I used the word *divorce* in the argument. I was so done with arguing and didn't want to spend the rest of my life continuing to fight the way we did. I also felt that we were the only couple with this problem, and everyone else had an amazing marriage. (I think this is the ultimate lie most couples believe when they're challenged with a tough time in their relationship.)

Because of this extremely bad argument, our pastor and his wife suggested that we go see a counselor to get some professional help. Though I was OK with the idea, I didn't click with the counselor we chose. We saw him on a weekly basis, and every time we did, I felt like he called out what I needed to change and would rarely tell Laura that she needed to change. I now know that this is usually how the guilty party feels.

I couldn't believe that I was the only one who needed to change. This was supposed to be a fifty-fifty relationship. That meant to me, *at the time,* that if I had something that I needed to change, then Laura would have to change something too. I grew up having a very bad temper, similar to Bob from my previous story. But I felt I had pretty good control over it. It was something I'd really worked on and had asked God to help me. My temper was what the counselor kept throwing in my face.

Around the third or fourth session, I felt he was really out of place with some of the accusations he made about what I needed to change. I kept my cool in the room, but I was either really hurt or just angry—I can't remember. We left the session and got in my truck. As we drove away, something Laura said set me off. I was driving down the highway at about sixty-five miles per hour, and I just lost it. I began yelling expletives over and over again. I drove very erratic and dangerously. The anger exploded inside, and I was not myself. I could actually feel it. As I acted out in this totally wrong manner, I was not only endangering Laura's life and mine but the lives of others on the highway as well. When we finally arrived home, Laura announced, "I will never ride with you again."

I can't tell you enough how remorseful I was—and at the same time, hurt. I felt that I'd been wounded by the counselor, but it gave me no right to act the way I did. I knew that what I'd done was wrong, but I didn't feel like it was actually me doing it. I was confused and upset and bewildered.

Over the next few weeks, our marriage seemed to get better—either that or we were just too busy with life to address our root problems. Laura had forgiven me for the way I acted, and we went on with things.

In August, our pastor recommended that we attend a marriage course. He and his wife, as well as other couples they knew, had taken it and said it was one of the best ones they'd ever attended. We thought we should probably go to see if it would help us repair our damaged relationship.

We signed up for the one-week course in November. Barry and Lori, the couple putting on the conference, asked if we'd be willing to facilitate a table with three other couples. All we had to do was make sure everyone at the table stayed on time with the discussions and that everyone had ample opportunity to speak. So, we agreed to be facilitators as well.

At that time, it seemed like our marriage was doing pretty well, and I was excited to go on a trip to California with my wife and get away for a week. But on the Tuesday before we were to leave, that all changed.

Laura, Raquel, and I sat down to dinner, and we were laughing and cutting up with each other. I don't remember what Laura said, but I took it the wrong way. I began to get angry on the inside, then I got very quiet and went over to the sink to wash the dishes.

Over the next few days, we didn't say much to each other unless we absolutely had to. By Friday night, I couldn't take it anymore. I asked Laura, "Why are we even going to this marriage seminar?"

"Because if we don't go to this, I don't know what else we're going to do," she said.

"Fine," I replied. "But we should contact them and tell them that we aren't in any place to lead a table."

Laura then said to me, "All we have to do is facilitate things to make sure we stay on time. It's not that big of a deal."

By Sunday, we were cordial with each other and got on our flight to California. With that, we were on our way to this seminar that was supposed to change our lives forever—yeah, right. We checked into the hotel and settled into bed. On Monday morning, we arrived before everyone else because they'd asked the facilitating couples to come early for instructions. After a few minutes of telling us how to lead our tables, I picked out two seats at our assigned table. This was a five-day conference and would start at 9:00 a.m. and end at 9:00 p.m. The only breaks were for lunch and dinner, and even then, you were to eat with the other couples at your table.

It wasn't long before two of the other couples showed up. The fourth couple that was supposed to be at our table never came to the conference. I wondered if they'd had a similar week before the conference and decided to skip this altogether.

Our conference leader, Lori, started the Monday session by welcoming us all to the "Love after Marriage — Nothing Hidden" conference. When she said this, I immediately thought, *WHAT? Nothing hidden? How did I miss that in the title?* I'd never noticed that, and now I was stuck there for a week. Other people were going to find out things about us that I probably didn't want them to know. What had I gotten myself into?

Lori spent the next couple of hours telling story after story of couples who had taken this seminar over the years, and many of them found the breakthrough they were looking for in their relationship. She told about the many hidden things that were revealed, like drug abuse, alcoholism, pornography, deep hurts, adultery, and even witchcraft. Bringing such things to light allowed the couples to find that breakthrough they needed. We sat through those first few hours and listened to story after story about couples who'd come with broken marriages and left healed. That's what I wanted, too, but I was very nervous about what we were in for and how deep we had to go to fix things.

After that first session, we went to lunch at a local Mexican restaurant with the two other couples. Laura and I had been prompted to talk about our life and what we wanted to get out of the conference. It was very good for us to share, and because we both were so open and real when we shared, the other two couples felt like they could be more open as well.

When we got back, Lori mentioned that there was a sign-up sheet where couples could write their names if they were interested in sitting on stage and allowing Barry and Lori to walk them through a spiritual breakthrough in their marriage. During each morning session, Barry and Lori chose one couple to go on stage to experience a spiritual marriage breakthrough. There was no way I was signing up for that!

On Tuesday morning, we all arrived for the first session of the day. Barry and Lori greeted everyone, then grabbed the sign-up sheet. They invited one couple to come on stage, who seemed fairly normal from all appearances, but the husband did look like a very serious tough man.

There were four chairs on stage. Barry sat directly across from the husband, and Lori sat across from the wife. Barry asked the couple to tell a little bit about themselves, like how many kids they had, the kids' ages, and what the couple did for a profession. If I remember right, the couple had been married for about fifteen years.

Barry asked them how he and Lori could help them. With this, both the husband and wife sat there and stared at each other for a few seconds. Then the husband looked at Barry and said, "I've had an issue with pornography for the last fifteen years, and we don't know how to fix that."

With that, Barry said, "Well, I guess it didn't take long to get to the root of the issue in this marriage." Barry and Lori went on to ask some more questions and discuss other things that might be happening in their relationship. I noticed the husband's countenance during this time. He was very direct, short, and looked very hardened.

After about a half hour, Barry asked the husband if he remembered the first time he'd seen pornography. The husband said no, he'd pretty much remembered it being around him his entire life but had no recollection of when he first saw it.

Barry then said that, together, they'd ask Holy Spirit to help him remember this. He asked the husband to close his eyes and said, "Holy Spirit, will you help me remember the first time I saw pornography?" With his eyes still closed, and after only about twenty seconds, the husband said, "OK. I'm there."

Barry asked, "What do you see?"

He said, "I see my dad sitting on a couch watching TV. A pornographic movie is playing."

With that, Barry asked, "Where are you in the scene?"

He answered, "I'm standing in my crib." At this point, most of the people in the room gasped. Barry looked at everyone and asked them to be quiet.

Barry continued, "How old are you in the scene?"

The husband said, "About three or four years old."

With that, Barry asked him to open his eyes, and they began to talk about what had just taken place. Barry told the couple that now that they knew the root of the issue, they could deal with getting this out of their marriage.

Barry asked if they would like to pray to have this removed, and they both said yes. He had them repeat a prayer after him to thank God for revealing the deep roots of the issue. Barry then said, "Today we nail to the cross the pornography that's in this marriage, never to be a stumbling block to them again." He continued with, "And we replace this area of pornography with the righteousness of the purity of Christ Jesus. We thank You, God, for restoring our marriage as it was meant to be."

With that, they were smiling at each other. From my vantage point, it looked like this was a totally changed person and couple. I could see the husband's demeanor transform to the point that he was smiling and his countenance was soft.

Barry asked him to do one more thing before they ended this session that had now been going on for almost two hours. Barry said to the husband, "Let's end by asking Jesus to come into the scene you first had."

Barry said, "Close your eyes and ask Holy Spirit to put you in the scene where you first saw pornography."

The husband closed his eyes, but this time he was so much more relaxed. He said, "Holy Spirit, please put me in the scene where I first saw pornography." After a few moments, he said, "OK. I'm there."

Barry then asked him, "What do you see?"

He replied, "The same as before. I see my dad sitting on the couch watching a pornographic movie on the TV, and I'm in my crib."

Barry then said, "Ask Jesus to come into the scene."

The husband said, "Jesus, will You come into the scene?"

Almost three seconds later, this tough, rough man began to laugh and giggle like a little boy. When we all saw this, we started laughing too. Barry asked us to be quiet.

Then Barry asked, "What do you see?"

The husband responded, "I see Jesus in the scene."

Barry replied, "Where is He?"

The husband said, "He's standing between me and the TV."

Barry asked, "What is He doing?"

The husband said, "He's making silly faces at me."

With that, Barry asked the husband to open his eyes. The man was a different person. I couldn't believe what I'd seen take place in him. I didn't know that letting go of something could change your entire demeanor.

175

Barry prayed over the couple and let them return to their table. Then he and Lori explained the three-step process for restoring a relationship:

1. Ask Holy Spirit to reveal something that was hindering their relationship.
2. Verbally nail that to the cross that Jesus died on.
3. Replace that with a truth from God.

Each of us would do the same thing at our table. We were to ask the Holy Spirit to speak a word to us about something that was hindering our marriage. Then, as couples, we'd walk through the three-step process to remove that hindrance and replace it with the truth.

Each couple would do the process with their spouse. The other couples would help by asking questions to get to the root of the issue that the Holy Spirit had revealed. The facilitating couple was to go first, and Lori said it should take about fifteen minutes per couple.

With that, everyone at our table bowed our heads and asked Holy Spirit to reveal a word that was hindering our relationship. I heard the word "control." When all of us had gotten our word, I was supposed to ask my wife what word the Holy Spirit had revealed to her.

I looked at Laura, and she told us her word. The other two couples and I asked Laura questions to get to the root of what the Holy Spirit wanted to remove from our relationship. It was amazing to see Laura experience a breakthrough in her life due to this process. However, the process took almost forty-five minutes and didn't leave much time for the rest of us. I looked over at Chad, the husband across from me, and he said, "I will only need five minutes," to which I replied, "I will do it in three." It would take me much longer than that, I can assure you.

Now Laura would walk me through the same exercise. But before she did, I felt I needed to ask Holy Spirit the question again. I prayed, "Holy Spirit, please reveal a word of something that needs to be removed from my life." This time, I heard the word "abuse" and told the group.

So, two words had come to my mind from the Holy Spirit—control and abuse. I didn't understand how these two words related to each other, yet I felt there was something that God wanted to do in me to help our marriage.

I closed my eyes, and the group began to ask questions about how control or abuse might be in our marriage or if I had experienced them in my life. I began to remember back to a few times that I'd felt verbally abused in my life. I mentioned that to the group, but I didn't really think that was the core of the issue.

Then I was taken deeper into areas of abuse in my life, and I remembered a time when I was almost sexually abused. I was about six years old, and the other person was about seventeen. I was in a room with him and a few other guys his age and another kid my age. He was lying on a bunk bed, and all the guys in the room were laughing and talking when one of them asked me to come over and do something I didn't want to do. When he reached out to force me, I ran out of the room, and they all started laughing. Before I got out of the room, he

177

told the other kid my age to do it as well. I don't know what happened to that kid after I left; I just know that this moment affected me for a time when I was younger—and probably carried over into my adult life. I said to the group, "It may be the abuse I felt when I was six, but I really don't think this is exactly the abuse that I'm supposed to address." Up until that point, I'd never told anyone this story.

Laura and the others kept asking me questions about what the words *control* or *abuse* could mean. Then I started to think about the things in our marriage that Laura knew nothing about—things that I'd kept hidden from her for years. I thought that if she ever found out about them, there'd be no recovery in our marriage. I thought, *I can't tell Laura about these things. I'm scared about how she would react.*

But this was exactly what the words *control* and *abuse* were in our marriage. I was trying to control an area of our marriage that I had abused. If I didn't let go of trying to control this, these issues and secrets would remain in our relationship. If I didn't do something now, there might not be another time.

I put my head between my hands with my elbows on the table and began to wrestle with the entire process I was going through. Suddenly, the story of Bob shooting the neighbor came to mind. Everything that I'd heard him talk about at chapel raced through my thoughts, and I got very scared. What had once been Bob's choice to let go and trust God now became my choice to let go and trust Him in this situation.

I heard God ask the same question that He asked Bob. "Am I the Lord of your life? Do you trust Me with everything that belongs to you, even your marriage?" With these questions bouncing around in my mind, I wrestled and wrestled with this decision in front of the entire group. It was only a few minutes, but it felt like a lifetime to me. Finally, I told God, "Yes, I trust You."

With my head in my hands and my eyes closed, I said, "You all don't know me. I'm not the same man I once was. I'm totally a different person."

Laura reached over and wrapped her arms around me. She said, "It's OK. No matter what it is, I'm with you." To me, Laura was the picture of Jesus Himself holding me and telling me it would be OK. At that moment, I made the choice to trust God fully and let go of that which was destroying my marriage. God had given me the opportunity to make a change and stop hiding. It was now my choice to be free from what I'd held on to for too long.

I turned to Laura, and with every word from my heart, I said, "You know I've traveled a lot with my work. In the early years of our marriage, I wasn't always faithful to you. I never had intercourse with another woman, but I wasn't faithful to you. I'm so sorry. Will you please forgive me?"

When I was finished, Laura looked at me and said, "Yes, I forgive you. It's OK."

We sat there and held each other. There weren't a lot of words or details in my apology. I simply confessed to Laura what I knew I needed to. Laura, in turn, didn't ask any questions. She simply responded like Jesus responds to us when we come humbly with our confession of sin to Him. She simply forgave me.

No bells went off, and I didn't feel the relief of a huge weight being lifted off my shoulders. I felt quiet. I'd simply trusted God to be my Lord over this situation, and He'd removed this burden from our marriage. Now there was nothing hidden in our relationship, and there never would be from that point forward.

Since that day, our marriage has never been the same. We have a renewed relationship and love for each other that makes me wish I'd done this sooner. Laura is the love of my life, and if I could, I would choose her all over again. I can't imagine my life without her. Yes, we still have disagreements like in any marriage, but now it's so much different. We really enjoy each other.

My decision to let go and trust God has transformed my entire life. Ever since, I've noticed many different changes in me. I don't get angry like I did before. It's been a long time since I've yelled at anyone. God has helped me to let go of things that bother me much more easily. I've also noticed a renewed confidence in trusting God as Lord in all areas of my life, as well as a deeper confidence in who He created me to be. Additionally, I love to pray for people because I know that God is who He says He is, and He can do what He says He can do. He is loving and caring and is waiting for us to let go of our way and trust that He has the best for us. These were not immediate changes, but they came about more and more over time.

In 2012, when I had my second stroke, I had a procedure to close a hole between the two chambers of my heart. If this hole wasn't repaired, then blood clots would continue to transfer from one chamber of my heart to the other, then travel to my brain—and I'd continue to have strokes. With the filling of the hole in my heart, I could now live out a healthy, long life.

During the months after the procedure, friends would joke that Jesus had filled the hole in my heart. They said this because that's what Salvation does for us. It fills the gap that we once had where sin could creep into our lives. Without Salvation, we'd experience eternal death in hell rather than eternal life with God in Heaven.

Since I was a young boy, I'd always gone to church and followed God, and I felt that I trusted God as my Savior from sin. I felt that I loved Him, and I had a deep desire to live for Him alone and to pursue everything He had for me. Many times over these years, I felt like I was missing something. I felt like I was just *doing* Christianity, but was I living my life as God intended me to live? There were things that I felt obligated to do, like telling others about Him, serving in some form at church, or even having a constant prayer life, in order to be in right standing with Him.

After reflecting on this for a long time, I came to the conclusion that the procedure to fix the hole in my heart was both a physical act that happened to me and it also was a spiritual act in some way. Something happened that day that changed my life forever that I can't quite explain. After that procedure, I had a desire to know God more fully than I'd ever desired before. I began reading through the entire New Testament to find out all that it could tell me about God's desire for how to live my life. I also began reading many books on how to live out this Christian life. Though I always lived for God and had invited Him to be my Savior when I was younger, there was something about this one event that led me to let Jesus be the true Savior of my life.

Our experience at the marriage conference, where I chose to make God the Lord of my life and trust Him fully no matter the consequence, showed me what it meant to live a life of total dependence and trust in God. He had now truly become the Lord of my life. When given the choice, I chose to fully trust Him and let go of the things holding me in a place where I didn't want to live.

Today, I understand what it means to accept Jesus as my Savior *and* the choice we have to fully make God the Lord of our lives, trusting that in all things, He will take care of us. The Bible says that "He will never leave you nor forsake you" (Duet. 31:6). Our choice to let go and make God the Lord of our lives is the greatest choice we ever have to make. It allows us to have peace in the decision, no matter the consequence of that decision.

Your Choice

I wrote this book because I believe life is about *LETTING GO* of the things that we know we need to release. You've probably heard the saying, "You came into this world with nothing, and you will take nothing with you when you die." You'll certainly have to let go of everything you've acquired in your life when you eventually die. Between the time of your birth and the time of your death, you'll have many choices to either hold on to things or let them go. And it's not just physical things; it's the areas of your life that, deep down inside, you know you need to release.

Just like Bob and me, there are times when we must choose. Bob had to come to the point that he wanted to trust God so much that it could have meant time in prison. He needed to let go of a hidden past that kept him from trusting God fully. In letting go, the result was that he was pardoned for what he'd done. His reward for letting go was knowing what it was to truly trust in God with all things and never having to look over his shoulder at his past.

It was similar for me. I wanted my marriage restored to what we both felt a marriage should be. Yet there were hidden things that I needed to let go of and confess to Laura. If we were to move forward with full purity in our marriage, I could no longer hide the sins that I'd brought into the marriage. I had to let go of what I was hiding and trust God as the Lord of my life. The result of doing this was a renewed marriage and a deeper love for my wife. But more importantly, this choice to let go of the hidden things taught me what truly making God the Lord of my life meant.

Now that you've read this book, what are you holding on to that you need to release? Is there an area where you feel you are stuck and you need to let go? Is it a relationship issue, a marriage that seems to always be struggling, an addiction that you can't seem to break, or an idea that you can't get out of your head?

I believe we all come to a point in our life where we know we need to let go and do something different, or else we feel like we're going to die. We can't see any more hope to break free from that which is holding us. You don't have to live this way! You were created to live a life of freedom from these things that hold you.

The Bible tells a story of four lepers who were about to die of starvation. They decided to let go of where they were, step out with as much faith that they could muster, and trust God for deliverance.

> *Now there were four men with leprosy at the entrance of the city gate. They said to each other, "Why stay here until we die? If we say, 'We'll go into the city'—the famine is there, and we will die. And if we stay here, we will die. So let's go over to the camp of the Arameans and surrender. If they spare us, we live; if they kill us, then we die."*
>
> *At dusk they got up and went to the camp of the Arameans. When they reached the edge of the camp, no one was there, for the Lord had caused the Arameans to hear the sound of chariots and horses and a great army, so that they said to one another, "Look, the king of Israel has hired the Hittite and Egyptian kings to attack us!" So they got up and fled in the dusk and abandoned their tents and their horses and donkeys. They left the camp as it was and ran for their lives.*
>
> *The men who had leprosy reached the edge of the camp, entered one of the tents and ate and drank. Then they took silver, gold and clothes, and went off and hid them. They returned and entered another tent and took some things from it and hid them also."* 2 Kings 7:3–9

These four men couldn't be with the rest of the people of Israel because of their leprosy. They were shunned by everyone and weren't even allowed to beg for food. There was also a major famine in the land, and the Israelites were on the verge of being attacked by a great army.

These four were the least of the people of Israel and had no hope of getting any help. Every outcome they considered seemed to lead to the fact that they would die. But they were tired of staying where they were in life. They would die if they stayed where they were, and the other two options didn't seem much better.

They came to the point of decision. Would they let go and trust that there was deliverance out there for them, or would they remain where they were and die? They mustered up enough faith to let go of where they were (a place of famine and death) and move to a place they wanted to be (a place that had food). And when they let go and stepped out with a tiny bit of faith, God moved on their behalf. They gained not only food and wealth but freedom for the entire Israelite army. Their decision to let go not only changed their lives, but it also saved the lives of an entire group of people.

Do you feel that you need deliverance from something in your life? As you read this, you may be thinking, *There has to be something better out there. I can't keep doing what I'm doing.* You feel like if you stay where you are, there's no hope for tomorrow. You may feel like the four lepers, that any decision you make will have a negative result. It may not cause your death, but the decision to let go looks like it will bring pain, not freedom.

I know that impulse decisions sometimes lead to negative results, and I'd never suggest you do something rash like walking out on your job or marriage. But I also know that if you've accepted Jesus as your Savior and trust Him as Lord of your life, He'll always be there when you step out in faith. You can let go of that which is holding you back and step into all that He has for you.

I encourage you to do what Bob and I did. Seek to find out if you're trusting God as the Lord of your life. Is there anything you need to let go of that's keeping you from living the life you were meant to live? The Bible says, "If you confess with your mouth 'Jesus is Lord,' and believe in your heart that God raised him from the dead, you will be saved" (Romans 10:9). If you're looking for salvation from your past or present, nothing will bring deliverance like trusting in Jesus as your Savior and Lord.

Once you've asked Him to come into your heart and forgive you for your past, and you trust Him with your future, then simply listen to hear what He tells you to do to let go.

If you're looking for salvation from your past or present, nothing will bring deliverance like trusting in Jesus as your Savior and Lord.

If you're still having a hard time figuring out what's holding you back from where you want to be in life, try doing what I did at the marriage conference:

1. Ask Holy Spirit what you need to let go of.
2. Let go of that thing in prayer by saying, "I nail (fill in the blank) to the cross of Jesus."

3. Then replace that thing with a truth from the Bible that's the opposite of what you nailed to the cross.

I can promise you this: When you truly make Jesus Christ the Lord of your life, He will always be there to catch you when you let go. He'll always see you through to where you need to be. It may not be easy, but life is so much better when you let go of your way and trust Him as Lord in every aspect of your life.

Like my good friend, Dr. Tom Hill, always says, "The ball is in your court." It's now your choice. Will you let go and enjoy all that life has for you through this amazing life with Jesus?

ACKNOWLEDGMENTS

This book has been written from so many experiences in my life. I always thought about writing a book but could not have done this without the help of so many people.

Thank you to my parents, who continued to show me what it truly meant to have a faith in God that would not fail. Thank you for encouraging me through the years to be more than I ever thought I could be. Without you, I would never have pushed myself to go after all that God had for me.

There are so many people who helped me write this book. I wish I could acknowledge all of them, but I want to acknowledge a few of you personally. Thank you to Dr. Tom Hill, who pushed and asked when I was going to write my first book every time I met with him. Thank you to Tom and Randi Kyle, who stood with Laura and me through some of the hardest years of our lives. We would not have made it without the two of you being so gracious and kind in helping us see Christ in every aspect of our life. Thank you to Nancy Erickson, The Book Professor®, who pushed me to write freely and openly those things that needed to be in this book. It took a strong woman like you to push me to complete this book and help pull out of me all that God wanted to say through this book.

ABOUT THE AUTHOR

Derrik Kassebaum has been married to Laura for over twenty-five years. They have two daughters, Elise and Raquel. Derrik and Laura are co-owners of three different companies, including Cosmos Corporation, their family-owned manufacturing company that makes health and wellness products for the pet industry. Since 1980, the Kassebaum family has worked to create a trusted pet brand throughout the US and seventy-three other countries. Derrik has traveled the world building multiple pet brands, and from 1989 to 2018, he was Vice President of Sales for the company. He now sits on the board of Cosmos Corporation.

The family's nonprofit organization, Gifts of Love International (GOLI), was started by Derrik's parents, Don and Barbara Kassebaum. This family-run organization oversees many different works in Guatemala and Haiti, as well as other parts of the world. In Guatemala, GOLI oversees Nino's Amados (a home for children), works directly with the care of over sixty-five churches, runs Gratia Institute (an accredited pastoral training center) and CCI (a nine-month intensive young adult development program), and provides ministry work to government officials through Pro Nation. In Haiti, GOLI oversees a work called Celebrate Jesus of Haiti that feeds eight hundred children a day, has a school of 325 students, and runs a clinic that provides free medical care to children ages seven and younger, among other things to help the people of Loganave Haiti.

Derrik has sat on many boards throughout the years, including the Barnes-Jewish Hospital Foundation. BJF helps people through the expense of medical care and treatment incurred by cancer treatments and other major medical expenses. Derrik and Laura also work with many other ministries around the world to help bring unity, resource in aid, and Kingdom Culture to these ministries. If asked what his gifting is, he will tell you that it is envisioning organizations, connecting people, and encouraging individuals to reach all that God has planted in them.